An Ordinary Child

The ups and downs of a
childhood stroll along memory lane.

Gillian
Edwards

Copyright

ISBN 978-1-915787-26-2

Grateful thanks once again to:

Biddles Books for printing
&
JD&J Book Covers for the cover design.

Acknowledgements

Growing up, we had a running joke. My Dad used to say to me…

'As you were so was I, as I am so you shall be…'

He was referring to weight. It was a phrase guaranteed to wind me up alarmingly, which he knew of course, and he would laugh at my response. The reason being, when I was a baby, he said I was fat, as I got older, I was very slim, whereas he had become more portly as he aged. I used to protest with my reply of '*I shall never be!*'

When he died, we each put a single rose on his coffin with a note attached. Mine said…

'As I am, so you were, as you are, I shall not be!…'

Just so I had the last word on the subject!

And a note, I wasn't slim for psychological reasons, I was just naturally very thin, loved exercise and wasn't very interested in food.

More than anyone, I would like to thank my husband and best friend Graham for all his support and love throughout everything I have done and achieved. I love you with all my heart.
♥

I would also like to thank every one of my friends who have contributed to my life just by being in it.
Some names have been changed.

We all make mistakes, it's part of being human. Forgiveness is two-way.

Dedication.

I dedicate this book to David Harris, who has been a big influence in this book. Indeed, he has a whole chapter to himself, and was a very good friend during my childhood. He made me laugh, we spent time together playing and he created many happy memories for being mischievous.

He also made me publish my books in paperback, as when I published my first book, it was just as an E Book. David contacted me and said...
'I want a proper book!'
Me: 'It is. It's a downloadable book.'
David: 'No, I mean a proper book, paper version.'
Me: 'Will you pay for it.'
David: 'How much is it?'
Me: 'I don't know, I'll find out.'

A couple of weeks later, and lots of internet searching, and phone calls, and design of a printable cover, in the right format...

Me: 'David, I have a proper book, it's going to print.'
David: 'Great, let me know when it's ready. I want the first two copies.'

And so, I got my book printed in paperback, and David had the first two copies, and once again, he has had a positive impact on my life.

Contents

An Ordinary Child
Prologue

I am Gillian Edwards- I am, An Ordinary Woman

When I was 27, I knew I was going to write a book. I knew what it was going to be called, and I knew the time to write it hadn't arrived yet.

Mum died just before my 18th birthday. I missed her dreadfully.

As I got older, I couldn't understand why things seemed to keep happening to me. I felt ordinary and as I looked around me, other people seemed to have their lives organised and sorted. I felt like I was always falling from one bad decision to another.

Older still, I had an image of me as a grain of sand, and saw that I was rolling down a snowy mountain gathering more and more snow, and gathering more and more speed, and as I felt myself spinning downwards towards the bottom of the mountain, I felt dizzy.

One day, when I was 38, my snowball hit a tree and burst open. I shook myself down, and walked away. I felt free and in control for probably the first time in my life. And so began the journey into living my own life and writing my book.

I am an eternal optimist. My glass overflows even if the bottom has fallen out of the glass. Going on a journey of self-discovery wasn't something I planned. It just happened and I experienced lots of fun, and lots of tears along the way.

Lots of people encouraged me to write it down and told me I should write a book, so here it is.

This is the second book about me and my life, and I hope you enjoy reading them. If you do, please write a review when you finish it.

Aged 27

I feel as though I have never really got on very well with my Dad. It is very important to know that he wasn't a bad man, he and I were just very different in many ways. We often clashed and didn't see life in the same way.

One day, I came home from work and I started to wonder why I didn't like him, and more selfishly, what would happen if he died. Would I be filled with remorse about our relationship, would I fling myself on his coffin having seen the light too late and unable to change things, would I have regrets about unsaid thoughts and feelings. I needed to know, what it was about my Dad I didn't like, and was it my fault.

Every day, I would come home from work, sit in the complete silence of my home, cover my eyes with my hands to block out any distractions, and think.

I began by thinking about how I felt now, and truthfully, I didn't really like him. So, I thought about a few years ago, and a few memories that stuck out for me, and thought about them. Was I to blame? Possibly. I am in my twenties and I can think of several reasons why it could be my fault.

I think some more, and slowly but surely, I develop an ability to 'travel back' through my memory, a bit like rewinding a film, and think about various incidents. I try to be objective, did I like my Dad then? If not, could it have been my fault? Possibly. Back a bit further with the film.

I get back to my teens quite easily and quickly. I have big, strong memories here as my mum developed cancer and later died just before my 18th birthday. Still, I didn't feel like I liked him, but as a teenager, and with the stresses we all suffered with Mum's illness, I could see that it could still be my fault.

Probably aided by the fact that Mum and Dad took lots of photos and cine films, having grown up with these picture memories, regularly looking at them kept the memories of the events very fresh, I become very adept at flying up and down my 'memory film' stopping at various points to replay the scenes, and no, still the same. I still don't really like him and I still think it could be my fault.

One day, I was reliving some events and suddenly realised, I was about 5 years old. Thinking of other events, I was probably around 8 years old.

All of a sudden, the answer came to me. It wasn't my fault.

I decided that 'Little Me,' wasn't responsible for making me like my Dad when I was so young. It was up to him to make me like him. Little children respond as much to non-verbal language as they do, verbal.

9

Again, I must point out, he wasn't a bad man, he wasn't abusive, he was a good provider and loved and cared for us as a family. We, (he and I) just didn't get on very well. I think people who knew him would agree he was a 'one-off!'

I felt the weight of responsibility of it all, lift off my shoulders and knew that if anything happened to him, I wouldn't feel guilty. It was all right not to see eye to eye and just because we were father and daughter, didn't mean we were akin in other things.

My Dad died when I was 33 and he was 66. It was 2 days after my birthday and he had a heart attack. I had spoken to him the day before he died and the chances of me speaking to him so close to his death was unbelievable. I had no regrets and I now think of him fondly.

Which brings me to the opposite side of the coin. In many other ways, we were very alike and had lots of things in common. Not unusual, as father and daughter, we were bound to, and he had a great sense of humour.

He had quite a strong psychic ability, as did Mum and on that level, we were often on the same wavelength, which used to annoy me. I used to feel, if I was on earth and Dad was on planet 'Jelly,' I would still feel he was irksome and up to something!

One thing I realised at the end of this trip down memory lane, is that although we often didn't see eye to eye, and often I didn't like my Dad, I wouldn't have changed him for another one, because I wouldn't have become the person I am today. He was, in many ways, a man of his generation.

If I could bring only one of my parents back for a day, it would be my Dad. He loved technology and gadgets, and would be amazed and excited to see and use the world of the internet, mobile phones, sat-navs, wi-fi and all the other things we all now take for granted.

My mum was a home-bird, low technology and would find the pace and waste that is part of the world today, very difficult.

Language Difficulties.

I'm told lots of children with older siblings can be slow at speaking. I was apparently one of them and I'm told I didn't speak a word until I was two years old. I don't know what the 'abnormal police' would make of that these days, but no one worried and one day I spoke.

Dad always used to say, 'You didn't speak a word till you were two and you haven't shut up since!' I said I had time to make up! But, when I did speak, to begin with I spoke my own language and only to my sister Christine.

'B'bonk Pea, the batty's come.' Was a particular favourite and stuck forever which meant, 'Come on Chris, the paper has arrived.' The newspaper was always referred to as the 'batty.' I struggled for many years to say 'car park' and called it the 'park-ark.' Sometimes, even now it still comes out as 'park-ark!'

Dad was an undiagnosed dyslexic and struggled even to spell both our names. 'Chris' became 'Cris,' Gill became 'Gil' or 'Jil,' and Mum being Freda Louise, was often called Lou by my Dad but spelt 'Lousie,' or 'Loo!'

Mum said she gave us both names that would shorten without sounding awful and was careful not to have our initials making a silly word. That was great thinking by her, but didn't help Dad with his dyslexia and nicknames. His favourite for me was Flopper. He said it started when I was learning to walk, and as I wobbled along, suddenly, I would flop down. I was called Flopper for many years. Sometimes, Flop for short! Mum would have presumably approved. Christine still calls me Flopper sometimes.

As time went on, Dad would misunderstand and misspell things which were often really funny. I remember one day as we were in our teens and Dad came home after going out for lunch to do with his work. He didn't like fancy food and was particularly unimpressed at the offerings at this lunch. 'Who's this bloke 'Gordon Blue' he grumbled to Mum. 'I don't like his food.'

Mum was confused and said 'I've never heard of anyone called Gordon Blue. Are you sure?'
'Yes, definitely Gordon Blue, hardly anything on the plate and all fancy stuff. It cost a fortune. Waste of money in my view.'

Mum thought for a while and eventually, realised. 'It's not Gordon Blue, it's Cordon Bleu! Very posh and upmarket.'

'Well, whatever his name is, I don't like his food!' Says Dad.

As I started to grow up, I was found to be left-handed. Taking after my mum's father, I was led to believe this was a good thing and I would become artistic and creative. I'm not sure what happened along the way, but if art means being able to draw, I failed.

I suppose I am quite creative in other ways, I can sew, knit, embroider, and put words on paper. I love the English language even though I don't know all the words in the dictionary and my ability to understand and explain the rules of grammar, by definition, is all but non-existent. I can speak and write it but I can't tell a pluperfect from a past participle.

Growing up left-handed in a right-handed world is a challenge. Nothing at all existed to aid us left-handers. Mum clearly recognised this and I distinctly remember picking up my knife and fork and Mum changing them over to be right-handed. The trouble is, she didn't do the same for spoons, plates, cups and glasses. So, even now, I struggle to lay a table properly and am likely to eat someone else's bread, or drink from someone else's glass. When it comes to dessert, it is an absolute challenge as I want both my fork and spoon in the same hand. My stepmother kindly bought me some of those 'splade' cutlery items, which is a fork, knife, and spoon all in one, but although this makes it easier, the knife bit is still on the wrong side for me to cut anything with. Mind you, when I give them to guests to use, they all seem to struggle with them too, so at least I feel akin!

Going to school meant I didn't know which hand to hold a bat, racket, or ball in, but that didn't really matter either since I was, and remain, hopeless at throwing or hitting things with an implement. Hockey was an exception as with the ball on the floor, I could hit it quite well and a big part of hockey was running so as a left wing I was in my comfort zone.

Writing in a book for a left-hander is also a challenge, we end up with ink all over the side of our hand as it drags across the words we have just written, and if it's in pencil on a hot day, we can rub out everything as we go across the page with a damp hand.

Many years later, the bank helpfully produced a left-handed cheque book. I was gleeful and used it for many years, but after a lifetime of living in a right-handed world, left-handed scissors came along too late for me. I can't use them. On the upside, I became ambidextrous at lots of things including ironing, painting, and cleaning, and can use both hands equally well. Computers, mobiles phones and I-pads make things much easier so although things have become better for left-handers these days by recognising it's not something we 'choose' we still find the world is dominated by a lot of right-handed gadgetry.

Whooping Cough.

When I was 3 years old, soon after receiving my vaccine, I contracted whooping cough. I remember it well. I would lie on the settee in the lounge, and every now and again, I would cough so badly it made me sick. I was poorly. Added to which I also had measles at the same time. Apparently not a good combination and from what I was told later, everyone was very worried about me.

In the midst of all this, I naturally lost a lot of weight as I couldn't keep anything down. The only thing I really wanted was lemonade. Part of Mum's family owned a pop factory. 'Green's' pop. It was very popular in the West Bromwich area and Dad used to go to the factory and collect it by the crate. We always had pop. If we felt poorly, we would be given warm lemonade as a tonic. We also had cordial, but I didn't like it. It gave me tummy ache, and it hadn't any fizz.

So, here I am, on my sick bed, 13 weeks in total, with whooping cough and measles, and Dad was moaning and complaining that every time I had any lemonade, I would sick it up again. I remember lying on the settee with mum crouched next to me holding a bowl whilst I was sipping lemonade. Dad said giving it to me was a waste of pop, and also a waste of money. Mum told him I should have whatever I wanted. It's the one thing I remember most from the whole time I was ill.

Once I had recovered, I was left with 'a weak chest.' Every year I would get a nasty cold and a terrible hacking cough. In those days, we also used to get awful foggy smog in the winter and Mum used to wrap a big, mustard coloured, mohair scarf around my face to help keep the cold and muggy weather from getting onto my chest.

Every night in the winter, I would put Vick under my nose and on my chest to help me breathe more easily. Even now, I always put Vick under my nose when I go to bed! (My husband loves it!)

One year, I was suffering a particular bad bout of a chesty cough and Mum took me to the doctor. He prescribed lots of fresh air and any activities that would strengthen my lungs. Thereafter, I was encouraged to go outdoors, run around as much as possible and get as fit as I could.

Personally, I can only applaud the invention of the whooping cough and measles vaccine. Whilst there may be arguments against it and everyone has their own opinion and experience, I am convinced that without it, I wouldn't be here to tell the tale.

The Facts of Life.

As children, my sister and I spent lots of time at 'The Fieldhouse's.'

Their house backed onto our garden so we could talk over the fence, albeit we couldn't see over it, and we would 'run round the corner' to visit. It took about 30 seconds.

Mrs Fieldhouse was Mum's friend. Mr Fieldhouse was a legend for the things he possessed in his impressive garage-cum-workshop, and they had 3 children. Susan, Paul and Janet.

Every year on or near Bonfire night, either we would have a bonfire, or 'The Fieldhouse's' had one. Theirs were great fun and there was always lots of warm winter food to eat. Jacket potatoes, Grey 'pays' peas and bacon with pearl barley.

They were one of the first people we knew to have a colour TV, and one of our favourite activities as children was to go round and watch 'Little House on the Prairie' each week and sob our eyes out! We couldn't get over the wonder of the colour and how it made everything so life-like.

As a very little girl, sometimes Mum would leave me with Mrs Fieldhouse, and she would let me help her polish the hearth with her. I've no idea where Mum would go, but I was very happy making the hearth sparkle.

At the various birthday parties held at 'The Fieldhouse's,' somehow or other, I got to sing my favourite song of the time, 'Show me the way to go home.' It went down a storm, helped by the fact that I sung it with a Yorkshire accent. It must have started after a recent holiday to our caravan, where I regularly came home with a Yorkshire twang. Everyone loved it and encouraged me to sing it again, but at some point, I became shy and embarrassed and refused to perform.

At subsequent parties, I was always asked to sing and after much persuasion, and a stool to stand on, I usually agreed, but only if Mr Fieldhouse left the room as I was shy singing in front of him. At home Dad used to laugh at Mum singing, so I think I always felt he would make a big thing if I was singing, so I never sung within his earshot. Strange since we all had such a big love of music. It was years later that I discovered Mr Fieldhouse used to stand behind the door listening to me sing.

Janet was somewhat older than us other girls, and Paul being a boy would join us if we were playing hide and seek or such games, but he didn't want to do girly things, so generally, it was myself Chris and Susie who played together and we spent many happy hours helped by the fact that they always had a menagerie of animals to entertain us and play with. Kim, the

15

Alsatian dog, had such a lovely temperament with us children, but a fearsome bark and teeth for those who dared to approach us and were unknown. Kim was the definitive canine that taught me to respect dogs, how to approach them, and not take them for granted. They couldn't speak our language, but they could bark, snarl, and bite if provoked, and would roll over if they felt happy to have their tummy rubbed.

We watched frogspawn grow into tadpoles and frogs, we saw kittens grow into cats, and a variety of puppies came and spent happy lives before nature took them away again.

One exception to this was Terry. 'Terry the Tortoise' to be more precise. We knew he had a lovely shell and by counting the rings we could tell how old he was. One day we decided we would get the olive oil out and give him a wash and brush-up. Armed with a little brush, he was dunked into the water in the sink, shell scrubbed gently and then we turned him over to do his tummy...

He seemed to have a little dent in his tummy and every time we rubbed it, he wriggled and some 'stuff' came out of his rear end. We rubbed some more, he wriggled some more, and more stuff appeared. Heaven only knows how much we rubbed and how much 'stuff' Terry produced, but eventually we gave up and polished him with olive oil and he looked all the smarter for it.

It was only some years later that we discovered we had been rubbing Terry's erogenous zone and the 'stuff' he produced was to make baby tortoises! Whether he slept for a week after, or ran off round the garden clicking his heels in his shell, I'm not sure, but he lived, and I believe at the time of writing, he is still with us none the worse for our handling, or rather mishandling, of him when he was much younger.

Keep The Noise Down!

One thing my Dad and I had in common was a distaste of loud noises. Dad was quite obsessed with noise.

One Christmas Mum took me shopping and we went into a record shop where she started to look at records. I was very confused as we didn't have a record player. She placated me by telling me she was buying them for Dad to play at his works social club where he played piano sometimes.

Christmas day arrived and we went into the lounge to find a sparkly new record player. We were so excited and Mum produced the records she had bought when we went shopping. My favourite was an album that had 'A walk in the Black Forest' and 'A white sports coat,' (and a pink carnation) and we played them over and over.

Dad wanted to put the speakers on the wall, so having drilled the holes for the brackets and hung them up, he then made several trips to our neighbour to see if he could hear the noise through the wall. The volume was turned up to a deafening level before Dad decided it was ok.

Listening to the new records at a lower level, Dad started to fidget. He could hear a funny noise and then spent ages fiddling with it before deciding the record player was making a funny noise so it had to go back. A few days later and we had another one. We went through the same process before he decided this one was the same, and after another two attempts at replacements he concluded it was a design fault so we had to have a new model. Thankfully this one made no low-level noises and we could all relax and listen to the records.

Some years earlier I remember standing in Mum and Dad's bedroom and saying to my mother. 'There's no such thing as silence is there Mum.' She was busy making the bed so just responded with 'Mmm.'

'But there isn't is there? Even when it's silent there's a noise isn't there?' I tried to describe the high-pitched sounds I could hear, but she clearly didn't know what I was talking about.

When I was very young, I suffered with earache from time to time and Mum used to put drops in my ears or gave me warm milk with a bit of brandy in, (Yuk!) I realised at a young age, that I didn't know what silence sounded like. If I went anywhere where the noise level was too high, like a party or a disco, I would suffer with painful ear-ringing and diminished hearing for a couple of days afterwards. I couldn't understand why no-one else seemed to be as bothered by it as I was. Many years later I discovered I suffered with tinnitus and it all made sense.

As I got older and had my own house, I also suffered the same annoyance of electrical equipment background noise that my Dad complained of, and similarly made sure I chose things that weren't noisy. When it is very quiet, I can hear all sorts of things, including flowers opening, and I hate hoovering because of the noise it makes and it sets me off hearing all sorts of imaginary noises like the doorbell ringing. Conversely, when there is a lot of noise, I can't hear anything much at all as all the noises merge together. I suspect that my Dad had similar hyper-sensitive hearing and this is why he was so obsessive about noise.

Meet My Family

I was born on 23rd March 1963. One of the coldest winters on record, although I can't remember it! I believe I was quite shy as a young child.

My mum was very close to her own father and her mother was a bit of a harridan. Mum was an only child and born in 1923. She was a West Bromwich Albion fan and used to go to all the home games with her father.

One November morning, my Grandfather walked out of his home and went to the Post Office to draw his pension. He never came home. Distractedly, he stepped out in front of a car and was hit by an unfortunate lady who was also a nurse. Taken to hospital, he had suffered fatal injuries and died a few days later, on 30th November 1963. He was 73. My mother was devastated.

She never got to say goodbye to him. Retired from work, he had been quite a figure in West Bromwich in his day, sitting on various boards. He was also chief borough gas engineer and had served as Chief Mason. He was also bestowed an illuminated address for his services.

He was left-handed too, and by all accounts a lovely and well-respected man. I can only imagine the trauma my mum must have suffered having a new baby to care for and losing her Dad all within a few months. I don't think she ever got over it.

My Dad was born in 1929. He was also an only child and was a practical man. He followed his father into working for the public works. The council as it later became. He worked as an electrician and our house was, funnily enough, painted the exact same colour green that the council used.

Our garden had the same geraniums and dahlias as seen in the local parks, and our washing up liquid often happened to be the same as used by council canteens. A gallon of Teepol lasted a long time although it didn't smell as nice as Fairy Liquid and was very watery. If you ever watched 'On The Buses,' that was how life was. If you could cadge something from work to help eke out the household budget, people did. Even in later life, Dad still drove with two galvanised buckets in the boot, and if he saw a lay-by with sand and gravel piled in it, as we often did, he would pull over and help himself to a couple of buckets.

Both families went to church, and my Dad played the church organ. Both my parents were classically trained pianists but whilst Mum played classics from music scores, Dad preferred honky-tonk type, more modern and played by ear. He regularly played for his works social club.

They got married in February 1958 and moved into our traditional 3 bedroomed semi-detached post-war house. It was a house that my mother loved. My sister was born in 1960, and my parents were together until Mum died on December 8th 1980. The same day as John Lennon was shot.

Dad's parents had a caravan in Bridlington. A few years later, in 1967, my second grandfather died. He was 66 and had suffered a brain haemorrhage. He and my Grandmother were planning to move to live in Bridlington having just bought a newly built bungalow. My grandmother decided to stay in West Bromwich, so the bungalow was sold and Mum and Dad took over the caravan. Consequently, we spent all our childhood holidays at the caravan and Bridlington and Yorkshire became a second home.

Moving House

Mum always wanted to live in the house we lived in. She watched it being built and when it came up for sale just as Mum and Dad were getting married, they were fortunate to have been able to buy it.

It was a traditional post-war semi-detached 3 bedroomed house. It had Crittall metal rectangular leaded-light square windows and I can still remember the noise and musty smell that emanated from Mum wiping them down in the winter as the condensation ran down the inside and landed in puddles on the ledge. In winter, the water turned to ice and often welded the net curtains to the window. By the end of the winter, as the rust started to show through the paintwork, Dad would then slap a coat of gloss paint on them to cover up the rusty marks.

In those days we also had summer and winter curtains, the winter one's were heavier to help keep the draughts out, the summer let the light in and were unlined so over time faded badly making them look stripy! As with most of our clothes, mum also made all our curtains. Later on, as her eyesight wasn't so good, I remember she bought a pair of curtains for the lounge and then spent months apologising and explaining her extravagance to everyone. She felt guilty about not making them.

As time went on, various things needed doing to maintain the house and Dad decided we should move. Mum didn't want to, she loved the house we lived in and despite many trips to view houses that were for sale, we didn't move. At one point, Mum and Dad even owned a plot of land on a newly built housing estate around the corner, but eventually, it was released and we stayed where we were. The problem with this, was that Dad didn't want to do any work on our house because he wanted to move, and Mum wouldn't ask him, because it opened up the whole debate again. Consequently, the house became a bit tired and jobs were done as a make do rather than to update and upgrade. We had two verandas on the back of the house that linked the kitchen to the garage. They were always really cold and housed the fridge, tumble dryer, washing machine, (boiler with an electric mangle,) spin dryer and an overflow cupboard for food. There was also a brick-built, full-height, built-in storage cupboard in each of the verandas. One housed 'stuff,' no-one ever used and smelt of old polished furniture, and the other one we used to hang our coats in and store the ironing board. It also had a little heater in it so we used it as a drying room sometimes. Outside was a brick-built shed which was Dad's domain. Full of his tools, electrical finery and all sorts of odds and ends, it also housed an air compressor. I really hated the noise of the compressor and was always frightened it would blow up. I still dislike air compressors.

Inside the house, we had a lounge and a dining room. We had coal fires and later, we had electric fires that sat neatly in the hearth with fake coals that glowed with orange lights. During the short working week and coal strike, as the electricity went off, we had coal fires again. Odd in a coal strike!

We did modernise from the piece of square carpet edged with lino, to fitted carpets, and in the kitchen, we eventually had some more modern fitted cupboards instead of the loose fitted unit and Formica table that we grew up with. We also had an under-stairs pantry, which I didn't like as it was often hiding some sort of creepy crawly. It's amazing to think how little we had in the kitchen but still managed to cook everything from scratch and have a fully functioning kitchen. Nowadays, we have huge kitchens full of gadgets and gizmos but so many people don't cook, preferring to eat out and have takeaways!

The height of kitchen gadgets for us came in the form of a hand-held Kenwood mini-whisk, and sometime later a toaster and a food processor.

The cooker had a gas lighter on the side of it and as you brought the handle upwards, it would spark and light the flame. We then used this to light the rest of the gas on the cooker. I remember when it changed to North Sea gas and a man came to fiddle with the cooker and afterwards, the gas lighter was disconnected as it produced a flame that a second world-war flame-throwing tank would have been proud of! They also apparently added a smell to the gas so it was easy to know if you had a leak or left it on by mistake, and also for some reason we were led to believe it was more difficult to gas yourself by putting your head in the oven than when it was town gas. I don't know anyone who tested this out though.

Our cooker also had a plate warmer on the top of it and we used to put the tea towels over it to dry them afterwards. Whilst I realise the Health and Safety laws would now ban such things, we managed never to set fire to anything. We were just more careful in those days.

I think we had a normal sort of home life, but like most families we had good and bad times.
My parents didn't go out in the evenings very much, Dad worked a lot in the evenings doing electrical work, and Mum sat in knitting and sewing. If Dad was at home, he was invariably in his shed doing things. As I mentioned, I believe he was an undiagnosed dyslexic so reading a book wasn't his thing.

He was a practical person and loved gadgets, as long as they were useful. (Something I have inherited)

At 10.00pm each evening he would come in from the shed and we would all sit quietly as we watched News at 10. Dad always had a cheese sandwich for supper, on brown bread. It didn't matter what he had done or where he had been or even how much he had eaten during the day, he always had his cheese sandwich.

He wasn't very adventurous with food and even chicken was a bit unusual for him. He liked beef, pork chops, boiled potatoes and tinned peas. On Mondays after he came home from work, he always had a migraine and would sit in the dining room on his own, and always seemed to have lettuce sandwiches on these days. We would try to be quiet 'as Dad had a headache.'

He suffered with his back and had a degenerative spine condition which meant his back 'went' every now and again, and he would walk at a funny angle for a while until he recovered. For this reason, he didn't want to give up his secure job with the MEB, in favour of going self-employed. Unfortunately, he didn't enjoy his work at the MEB in later life, so I suspect this was the reason, every Monday, he had a bad head.

Dad was a curious man and open to listen to all sorts of ideas. One example of which was when he heard about a man who was doing the rounds at various churches locally, 'healing the sick and crippled.' Dad wasn't expecting to have a miracle bestowed upon himself, but just in case, and moreover, to see exactly what it was all about, he and Mum went to one of the meetings. It was at the Bethel Chapel in West Bromwich.

They took their seats and as things got going watched the man minister to several people. Placing his hands upon their head, he declared they were healed and whatever ailment they had, had gone. Astounding!

Next came a man on two sticks. He struggled to walk to the front and the minister placed his hands on his head and declared him to be healed in a loud booming voice. Then, he said to the man, you do not need those sticks, you can walk, and kicked away his sticks, whilst pushing him backwards onto the floor. The man crashed to the floor and the minister said, 'get up, you are healed!' Unfortunately, his miracle-working literally seemed to have fallen flat as the man couldn't get up again. Flailing around, the minister started shouting at him, 'get up man, you are healed.' Again, he failed to respond and eventually people in the audience had to rescue him. Dad decided he had seen enough and this was one miracle he could live without and they left quietly.

Occasionally, Mum and Dad would go out to 'play Chinese Chequers' with our neighbours and some friends. Nan, (Dad's mum) would come and babysit. We didn't mind as Nan was good company and we always had a good time with her. Mum would usually wear her 'best dress.' It was a plain mustard shift dress, and she wore a fur collar around the neck with a brooch to secure it all. I always thought she looked beautiful. She often wore a pair of wedge mustard mules which matched the dress perfectly.

Grandma, (Mum's mother) was a different kettle of fish, she was prickly and made Mum agitated. She had some wonderful phrases to make us all feel the weight of living was a trial to be endured rather than enjoyed. Things like, 'I don't know what we've done to deserve all this.' Or 'He's really dropped his clog on us' which was always said whilst looking upwards towards heaven, with a big dose of 'I can't believe I've come to this, I won't be here much longer' spoken with dewy eyes for added effect, she was a real joy to be around!

Christmases were a particular favourite for misery!

Christmas Cheer, Every Year!

Before I carry on, I don't want you to think life was miserable. It's just that a lot of the things I remember were. We all tend to remember really happy or unhappy events, the day-to-day living is mundane and unremarkable. In later life we look back at them with amused sentiment. Lots of the things that happened have a comedy value to them, and one thing I really do have in common with my Dad, is a sense of humour.

After the two Grandfather's had died, we had the two grandmothers come to spend Christmas day with us each year.

The day would start off happily enough, my sister Christine and I would be agog with all our presents and excited with a new dress or outfit to wear, new slippers and nightwear, and lots of toys to play with.

Preceding Christmas, every year, the four of us, Mum, Dad, Christine and I, would go off into Birmingham on the train, and go straight to Lewis's department store to queue all the way up the stairs to see Father Christmas and go around the grotto. Sometimes we would go straight to the restaurant on the top floor first and fight our way to get some food and get a table. We would then go to the toy department and Mum and Dad would surreptitiously find out what we would like from Father Christmas. I remember being overawed by the rocking horses, and a huge dark teddy bear that was there each year.

After the toy department, we would wander down the various floors and look at all the lovely things there were to buy. We would pour over the Chinese rugs, gaze at the pretty crockery and glassware, and Mum would wander around the ladies department looking at camel coats. She really wanted a camel coat and I was always confused as to whether it was a real camel.

Eventually we would end up in the luggage department where we used to love looking at the old-fashioned type trunks that were for sale. Full of drawers and hanging space, we imagined going on a long voyage, accompanied by your own beautiful trunk.

Like lots of men, Dad really didn't like shopping. He tolerated it at Christmas, and on holidays he would amble along outside while the three of us went in and out of the shops or browsed through the windows. He did enjoy browsing gadgets and electrical items and I'm sure if he was alive now, he would have an I-pad, and be hooked up to the internet and interactive TV.

One Christmas, after a particularly long wait to see Father Christmas, along with a full-on scrum to get some food and a crush through the toy department, we wandered back into the quieter departments as usual. Out of the blue, Dad blew a fuse.

Whilst we were admiring the Chinese rugs, Dad suddenly said, 'why are you looking at those, we aren't going to buy one!'

Mum saw red, and frogmarched us girls out onto the stairwell. Descending the stairs, at each floor she announced, 'Glassware and china, we aren't going to buy any of those, no point in looking.'

Next floor she said, 'Electrical, we aren't buying any of that, no point in looking.' She did this at every floor, until we got to the ladies wear, where she announced with a squeak, 'Camel coats, we aren't going to buy one of those, so there's no point in looking.' With tears in her eyes, and gritted teeth, we went home. Dad, unusually, was looking rather shame-faced. Chris and I were upset, not least because we rarely saw Mum and Dad argue.

Next year was business as usual and we all looked at the Chinese rugs and camel coats in peace!

One year, we were due to go into Birmingham and a week before, the Birmingham pub bombings happened. Everyone was shocked and stunned by it all. We assumed we would not be going to see Father Christmas, but Dad being Dad, had other ideas. He told us we weren't being threatened by it, the chances of it happening again were very remote and with all the extra police security, we would be safer than ever in Birmingham.

So, off we went. Unsurprisingly, other people didn't feel the same as my Dad, and Birmingham was eerily quiet. We didn't have to queue to see Father Christmas, there were plenty of tables in the restaurant, and there were very few shoppers in the toy department. We did everything we normally did unimpeded by crowds of shoppers and came home early. It is an experience and feeling I have never forgotten.

Christmas day would arrive and after opening our presents, Mum would cook dinner and Dad would take Chris and me to go and fetch the grandmothers. Nan was always happy to see us and then we had to go and get Grandma.

We would all try and be upbeat and happy, and she would put on an air of 'doing her best' to pretend not to show how miserable she was, but succeeded in looking the complete opposite!

By the time we got home, dinner was well underway and we would all sit down to eat. Crackers and party hats completed the scene and we all ate. Afterwards, washing up would be done and we would all sit down to watch the Queen's speech at 3.00pm.

Following this, the two grandmothers would have a good weep and wonder 'how it all came to this.' Their men were no longer here to enjoy Christmas and that made it all rather miserable. Then they would fall asleep and Mum would start to prepare tea. By the time tea was served, Mum had been testing the sherry for the trifle to calm her nerves and we would then all sit and eat. A photo would be taken, where everyone looked strained and drained, and before we knew it, it was time to take the ladies home. Nan was dropped first as she lived nearest, then Grandma.

In later years, Grandma lived in a care home and would spend all the time going back telling us how awful it all was. One thing she did seem to enjoy were street lights. She was always fascinated by the amount of them along the roads and found them as beautiful as Blackpool illuminations.

By the time we got home, Mum was exhausted. Mentally, emotionally and physically, and a little bit squiffy from the sherry.

Both the grandmothers had birthdays close to Christmas, one in January and one in February. So, we would repeat all of the above twice more, without the Christmas presents, in quick succession.

As time went on, it appeared the two ladies were having a bit of a competition. One of them told the other how much they were going to leave to Chris and me when they died. Not to be outdone, the other one added on some extras. At each get together, the list would get bigger, the amounts would get larger and eventually, they were both apparently able to leave us more than they actually owned.

Dad then added a new ritual facet to the 'dropping off the grandmothers.' On the way back he would say to us,

'If either your Nan or Grandma die and leave you anything, you do know that it really belongs to your Mum and me and you must give it back to us don't you.'

'Yes,' we would dutifully reply.

We hadn't the faintest idea of what it was all about really as we were too young, but we knew the answer was yes, and Dad seemed happy with the answer.

As many of us remember, TV was a strange creature when we were young. No colour TV's for many years and our TV took ages to warm up and produce a picture. Again, we were lucky and we had two black and white TV's. We could also tune into the radio with them. Who'd have thought it! Funny how it all changed and is now reinvented and back again. At the end of the night, after news at 10, the TV would end and as it closed down the national anthem would be played and we would watch the white dot until it disappeared to be replaced by a loud whistle to remind you to turn it off. Daytimes, when nothing was being broadcast the test card would be shown. The picture of a little girl with a clown and a blackboard is something we all grew up with and I was regularly asked if I was the little girl on the test-card as I was the spitting image of her.

Sundays were a bit miserable in many respects. TV didn't start until around 5.30 and was confined to Songs of Praise and Stars on Sunday, another religious programme, followed by something like Upstairs Downstairs, or World at War, and the news. We weren't allowed to play outside, as it was considered disrespectful. There was also no washing clothes allowed on a Sunday for the same reason. Monday was wash-day. We had a bath and washed our hair ready for school the next day and were early to bed to prepare for the week ahead.

On the upside, Sundays was the airing on the radio of the new top twenty and we would listen to it avidly to see what the new number one song was. As we got older things improved and daytime TV arrived on Saturdays where Noel Edmonds' Multi-Coloured Swap-Shop and Tiswas graced our screens.

As we got older, we were allowed to stay up later on Saturday nights so after Dad went to bed, Mum, Chris and I would stay up and watch films from the 'Hammer House of Horrors.' Not a good idea for me knowing my lively mind would turn anything into a nightmare, but with Mum to keep it all objective, Chris and I would hide behind our hands and peep through as some poor unfortunate would be mangled and terrorised by some ghoul or another. Mum and Chris were really good at knowing the names of the actors but I was hopeless at it.

One Christmas, we were thrilled as we had recently had a colour TV. Mum went into a spin, believing that Grandma would make her life miserable being so decadent and wasteful buying a colour TV. She got so agitated Dad moved it into the garage and put the old black and white one back for Christmas day. Once Grandma had been taken home Dad brought the TV back into the lounge, switched it on and BANG! It blew up. Condensation had built up inside the working mechanisms and it exploded. Mum burst into tears, Dad burst a blood vessel and the contents of the sherry bottle went down significantly.

A couple of weeks later and it was the start of the birthday re-run. Dad had had the telly repaired and put his foot down. Grandma could like it or lump it, but he wasn't moving it out.

Grandma arrived and the TV was switched on. We all held our breath and waited. Grandma peered and leaned forward to get a better view before declaring, 'Oh, that is a beautiful picture. What a lovely TV set!' We all breathed a sigh of relief.

Mum

Mum was lovely. I would say that because she was my mum. But she was a lovely person in her own right and everyone liked her. She had a good upbringing and had her standards. She wasn't a snob, but she like to do things properly and language was one of them. She had a soft black-country accent, and this only deviated when she answered the telephone and turned into some form of 'Mrs Bucket.' In fact, in those days lots of ladies spoke in a completely different fashion on the telephone. I have no idea why, but it may have been due to the fact that a telephone was a big luxury item and the voice you used was in deference to the reverence of the equipment!

Answering the telephone was always done by quoting your number, to simply say 'Hello' was considered rude and we were told off if we got it wrong.

We were lucky, we had a whole telephone line to ourselves. Supply and demand meant that for lots of people, they could only have a parti-line. It was a shared line and you had to make sure your shared line was free before you used it. If you were unlucky and got a parti-line sharer who had verbal diarrhoea, it was hard work getting the opportunity to use the phone.

We were taught to speak properly using correct grammar. We went 'to' the shops, not 'over' the shops, we went 'across' the road, not 'over' the road, and we went 'to' the town, not 'up' the town.

Liquorice was pronounced 'Liquoriss,' not 'Liquorish,' (which was a drunkard) and although the OED has updated some of its pronunciation acceptance since then, I am sure my mother would not have approved and deemed it as acquiescing to the lazy! She had worked as a secretary including time as a legal secretary and language was important.

Mum was adept at many things. She cooked everything. There wasn't much choice not to in those days. I remember the first time she 'bought' a ready-made Victoria sponge cake and she spent a long time apologising for it and making sure we didn't tell anyone since it was such a lazy thing to do and outrageous waste of money.

She made all our clothes. Knitting, crochet, sewing were all skills she possessed and it was very comforting in the evenings to listen to the gentle click-clack of her knitting needles as some wonderful masterpiece emerged from a ball of wool.

I only remember one failure of her knitting. She made herself, my sister and me a Fair-Isle jumper. It was off white Aran, with all sorts of lovely colours around the yolk of red, yellow, green and blue. They all looked beautiful and not an error of a stitch to be seen. Unfortunately, in the process of changing coloured yarns to form the pattern, the yolk had become tightened and so when we put them on, the lower half of the jumper would ride up and end up around our neck. She was really cross, but after so much effort, she refused to undo them and made us wear them. We were constantly uncomfortable and had to keep pulling them down. We were both glad when we grew out of them!

She made up for this one error with lovely patterns, complex Aran and up to the minute modern knitwear. When we grew out of them, she would unpick them and reknit into something new.

She gave up work after having us girls and stayed at home to be a housewife and full time Mum. Most ladies did in those days and I am so glad she did because it meant I got to spend the biggest amount of time possible with her before she sadly died so young.

One November day, Mum was very upset and it was so rare to see her cry, it was quite distressing. I was only young and Dad said it was because it was the anniversary of the day her Dad had died and she was missing him. I overheard him say to her, 'When your Dad died, a big part of you died with him.' I think he was right.

One of the consequences was my mum's mother, 'Grandma Green,' was a miserable, cantankerous, harridan and she made Mum's life miserable. Mum suffered with her nerves and anxiety and her mother was, in my view, the major cause. Mum couldn't do right for doing wrong with her and she was very jealous of anything Mum did or had. With the loss of her own father to keep Grandma in check, it all fell onto Mum's shoulders.

Dad wasn't seen as being good enough for Mum. This wasn't very fair, (although Dad was a bit of a one off!) He didn't have the same social skills that Mum had, but he came from a normal family. Both Mum and Dad had a good sense of humour, something I have happily inherited. Dad's humour was more dry and edgy, and he had a big sense of mischief.

Mum taught us all our household skills, cleaning, washing, ironing, cooking and food preparation. As I have got older, I am truly grateful and feel well blessed to have learned some of these skills which are now either back in fashion or seen as clever. I can gut a fish, cook a Sunday roast, bake cakes, pastry, biscuits, sew, make clothes and knit. Not necessarily all used on a daily basis, but I can do it. Having said all that, we didn't do much when we were little. Mum did everything for us. She said she wanted us to enjoy our childhood without lots of chores. Something she had missed.

32

She used to tell us stories of how when she was young, she would go to watch West Bromwich Albion with her Dad, but that she always had to clean the back step beforehand and it would often make them late. Grandma was uncompromising.

Not that we were spoiled. We weren't poor, we were never cold, hungry or without clothes, but my parents, and especially Mum, who was a few years older than my Dad, were brought up through the war years. Make do and mend, waste-not-want-not and using everything wisely was how we were taught to live.

Our house was comfortable. No central heating in those days and no double glazing so it was always quite draughty. Dad used to say you need at least one change of air in a room every hour to stay healthy. I think none of our generation had any problems with that!

I was lucky, in that having had whooping cough, I needed to be kept warm in winter and so an oil-fired radiator lived at the side of the bed to help keep me warm. With a hot water bottle and electric blanket too, bed was always warm and toasty in the winter.

We also had a convector heater and at night Mum used to leave a light on to help stop my nightmares. It was designed as a ship and the light glowed through the sails. I really loved this lamp.

Bath-time at home for us children was often a cold and chilly affair. The water would be heated by immersion heater and would take quite a long time to reheat, so if you ran a bath and it was too cold, it was a battle to get it warm again. Usually, we shared a bath or at least shared bathwater and the cast iron bath always took a lot of heat out of the water. We were rewarded though by copious amounts of bubble bath. 'Matey Bubbles' was a favourite and 'Crazy-Foam' was a soapy based product that we could spray on our faces and heads to make beards and funny faces.

My sister and I shared a bedroom as we grew up. Sometimes we would take it in turns to climb into each other's bed and snuggle down to sleep. Dad hated it. Even now, I have absolutely no idea why! If he caught us, we would get a smack. It's one of the few times Dad smacked us, normally just the fear would keep us in check, but for some reason we used to break this rule regularly and we would often get caught. Whoever had gone into the other's bed was the one who got the smack, so to keep things fair, we would take it in turns as to whose bed we would sleep in. Strangely enough though, I have a photo that Dad took of us happily cuddled up together in my sister's bed one night and so it seems on this occasion, we got away with it!

Grandma Comes To Stay

Grandma, suffered very severely with both osteo and rheumatoid arthritis. Her knees were hugely swollen and bent, and she had a very bent spine. (All she needed was a broom to complete the whole scene!) She was bad-humoured and as I have said, led Mum a merry dance.

Struggling to cope with living alone, she sold her house and put her name down for a place in a new old person's residential home that was still being built. After the house was sold, and before the home was finished, she came to live with us.

To begin with my sister and I were quite excited, but the atmosphere became tense as time progressed. When Mum went out shopping, Grandma would complain about how long she had been out and what she had been doing for so long, having left her on her own. Mum became increasingly stressed and almost stuck in the house. I don't know how long she stayed with us, but eventually, the home contacted us to say they had a place for her. Dad said he was determined she was going to go, although by this time she was keen to stay with us.

The home she moved to was lovely. She had her own room and it was all very modern. Grandma didn't like it and moaned and complained constantly about how awful it was. We used to go and see her every Monday, and from week to week, Mum was in various states of anxiety.

Mondays, were awful. Mum was always agitated, Dad was unpredictable, in that Mum was always worried he would blow a fuse and shout at Grandma about the way she treated Mum. Chris and I were bored having to go and sit in the home and listen to Grandma repeating herself and moaning to Mum.

Her favourite expression was, 'The food here is awful. No variety, we have the same thing every day and it all ends up in the pig-bin. I haven't eaten anything for days.' She would add in sobs and sniffles mopped gently with her hanky as her dewy eyes took on a sad hang-dog expression.

'I can't believe I've come to this!' was another regular phrase she used.

'If your Dad could see me now, he'd turn in his grave. Not to worry, I won't be here much longer.'

Dad, Chris and I really hoped she wouldn't. Mum just looked fearful and worried about the food, took her sandwiches which Grandma would eat noisily as the food rattled around her mouth as her false teeth were loose. Eventually, Mum spoke to the staff in the home who were really kind to her.

They told her Grandma had a very healthy appetite, ate all her food and invited Mum to drop in anytime she liked, at any meal time to see what the food was like. She did and without Grandma seeing her, she realised that Grandma was spinning a yarn. Mum found it difficult to believe Grandma was so cruel.

Tuesday's brought relief as it was another Monday survived and another six days until the process was repeated. Wednesday to Friday were better and then the wind-up to Monday began all over again.

If we were going to go on holiday, Mum would get in a complete flap working herself up to telling Grandma we wouldn't be going for a week or two. Grandma, would bemoan how 'I never see anyone from one week to another, unless you come.' Completely untrue, but made Mum feel guilty again. It all sounds so clear on paper, but living this life for Mum was very real and very stressful. Emotional blackmail is horrible and seemingly all of this got too much for Mum to cope with and she took some solace in the sherry bottle.

Two things I remember in the lead up to all this coming to a head. One is that, when I used to come home from junior school, Mum would speak in a bit of a funny voice. The other was she would smell of Parma violets. Sometimes she would ask my sister to run across to the shops to buy some Parma violets, and she would suck on them to presumably get rid of the smell of alcohol.

In the evenings when Dad was in his shed, Mum would walk round to the off licence at the pub around the corner. She would hand over her sherry bottle and they would fill it up. I loved going as I got a packet of cheese and onion crisps or nuts and somehow knew not to tell Dad where we had been. I am also aware she used to wrap empty bottles in newspaper and smash them with a toffee hammer and then put them in the dustbin outside, so seemingly she had more than one sherry bottle.

Dad Finds Out

Inevitably I suppose, Dad eventually found out about Mum's drinking problem and it all went up in the air. I'm not sure how old I was when it all happened but I was still at primary school and I think I was probably about 8 or 9. I don't know how it happened but my memory of it is that one Saturday, something was going on. Mum was in the lounge and Dad sent Chris and me into the veranda to play. He told us to stay there and we were both nervous.

After some time, he came into the veranda and said, 'I'm going to take you in to see your mum. Your mum is upset but I want her to see you both. Don't ask anything.'

I started to tremble and was immediately nervous and anxious. We went into the lounge and Mum was sitting sobbing. I instantly went to her as I was so upset to see her like it. Dad was very hard and told me not to go to her and pulled me away.

He said 'Your mother is drunk' and turning to Mum he said 'If you carry on like this you will lose your children.'

His tone was horrible. I was petrified. I had no idea what it was all about and was scared that either Mum was going away or we were. Dad sent us back to the veranda and I was in tears. Christine was upset too, but I just felt like I'd been kicked and thrown out of safety, into despair.

Next thing the doorbell went. I can't remember which it was, but a psychiatrist came and a priest. I'm not sure if they both came on the same day or not.

The rest is a blur. I know Mum was taking Valium or Librium for a time and she had a pretty tough time but other than the fact that there was no alcohol in our house for many years, life went back to normal.

I'm don't know whether I think Dad did the right thing or not. He undoubtedly did what he thought was right to shock Mum into doing something about her drinking but the effect it had on me was horrible. I didn't understand enough about it all and just felt very frightened and anxious as a result. I can only recount it from how I felt it as a child. In later years, I also realise that Mum still had a drink and kept it from Dad, but I also know that it wasn't a habit that was out of control, and in later life she and Dad would sometimes go out to a country pub and have a drink together.

My opinion looking back now is that Mum had a drink problem for a while, due to the stress caused by her mother. I don't believe she was an alcoholic as in later years she could happily have a drink and not have any problems whatsoever. I talked to several people who know about such things as I got older to see what they thought and they all said they didn't believe she was an alcoholic. In any event, it served to show just how unhappy life had become for her. I don't judge her in any detrimental way. It was a sad and difficult time for everyone.

Dad was never a big drinker. He only really liked cider which wasn't difficult as he was highly allergic to beer of any sort. In those days, we would occasionally buy shandy-bass from the chip shop when we were on holiday, which contained 0.5% alcohol and he couldn't even drink that. On the very rare occasions he was caught out he would have a fairly violent reaction to it hanging over the sink making all sorts of groaning noises as saliva poured from his mouth.

Unsurprisingly, growing up, I wasn't keen on alcohol. Yes, I got over it, will come the cry from those who know me, but until my late twenties, I preferred a glass of milk, (very unfashionable nowadays, in fact almost a crime to the non-dairy movement!) or lemonade. Thankfully, I can happily take it or leave it.

Bridlington

We were very fortunate. We had a big caravan, a big car, lots of holidays and days out.

As I said, holidays were spent in Bridlington. We had an Austin Cambridge, which Dad inherited when his father died, and later a Morris Oxford. Both of them had springy suspension and leather seats.

I had travel sickness!

Every time we were ready to travel, I automatically felt sick. I was given the anti-sickness pills, and even the smell of them made me feel ill.

By the time we got to Sutton Park, around 6 miles from home, I was already feeling ill.

'Are we nearly there yet?'

'Not far.'

Another few miles... 'Are we nearly there yet?'

'Not far.'

I would try and distract myself and curl up on the back seat and go to sleep. The tablets helped.

Four and a half hours later, several loo stops for Dad, (he seemed incapable of going past a toilet without feeling the need to visit it,) and we would be near our destination and we would then compete as to who could see the sea first.

Not that leaving home wasn't enough of a trial. Mum would rush around the house like a whirling dervish prior to any holiday. Beds were changed, the house was cleaned and scrubbed, and then the packing had to be done. Working out everything for all four of us, Mum used to get herself in a bit of a spin. She had a list of things to pack and ticked them off until the list was complete.

Dad would put the roof-rack on the car, wrap the suitcases in polythene and with food and other essentials, the car groaning under the weight, off we would go.

The final act before leaving was Mum going from top to bottom in the house emptying a can of fly spray into all the rooms. The smell was awful and I have no idea what she thought was going to invade us while we were away, but unsurprisingly only a few dead flies and a faint acrid odour met us on our return, at which point the windows and doors would be flung open to 'air the house.'

I always hated arriving anywhere, and this is something that extended until very recently. The reason is that after 4½ house in the car, I was warm and cosy. Arriving at the caravan which was always cold and soulless was too much of a climate change for me. With no speedy means of heating, it seemed to take forever to get the fire going and the warmth to penetrate the cold uninsulated caravan. Going out anywhere was the same, going from warm and cosy into the cold I always found unpleasant.

The rewards, however, were worth it. The beaches at Bridlington are beautiful. Long, gorgeous stretches of beautiful golden sand. There was, and still is, a proper working harbour and the wild North Sea to liven it all up. Contrary to popular belief, the sun does shine and it is possible to sit on the beach and dip in the sea, (which being the North Sea is freezing cold.) But, you can't guarantee the weather so in our day, a wind break was essential, along with a big woolly jumper.

'You are here to enjoy yourself, and enjoy yourself you will!' Dad would say, laughingly.

Actually, we did. We walked for miles and miles along the cliffs, over the moors, and visited almost every inch of Yorkshire. We had lots of picnics, curled up sandwiches, soggy crisps, a biscuit and a flask of tea, all the more tasty for the plastic cup.

We rarely stayed around the caravan, we were always out exploring. The fresh sea air used to knock us out and we often used to go to sleep listening to the low groan of the fog horn.

At the caravan, we were cooked a proper, full English breakfast. Bacon, egg, mushrooms fried bread, sausage, all cooked in lashings of lard. 'It will keep you going all day,' we were told. But for me, it was not very appetising. I wasn't used to eating a big meal so soon after waking up and often it was a struggle to get down.

At home, we didn't eat breakfast. Not for any reason particularly, we just never wanted it. I used to have a cup of milky tea and then rush off to school. No breakfast meant a longer lie in bed and I could get from bed to primary school, with appropriate ablutions, and drink my tea, in 20 minutes.

One morning, I didn't want my breakfast. Dad said I had to eat it. I got stressed and didn't want it even more, Mum said leave it, Dad said eat it, so I ended up forcing it down. Almost before I had cleared the plate, it came flying back up again and went all over the table, and even better, all over Dad! Mum looked smug, I felt ill, and Dad never made me eat breakfast again if I didn't want it. We were late going out that day!

We visited some lovely places, and many, I still love. Probably my most favourite of all was, and still is, York. There was so much to do there even then. The Shambles, the Minster, the railway museum complete with the royal coach and the Queen's water closet, and my personal best of the best, the York Folk Museum. In those days, it was a mock-up of a Victorian street, with shops and a proper horse and carriage. The horse was a real taxidermy horse. I loved it and used to run to stroke him. It was the highlight of the day.

Through Thornton-le-Dale, Hutton-le-Hole, occasionally visiting Castle Howard, we wandered across the moors to see the golf balls that were Fylingdales early warning centre, on to Whitby, there were so many things to see and enjoy.

Another unique place we used to visit was the ancient but still 'living' Staithes. A bit like a real-life Popeye's village, where the houses were all higgledy-piggledy. Some were so close together, people could reach out and touch the hands of those opposite. A very steep road led down from the top of the village to the sea. Unsuitable for motor vehicles, and hard work for the legs, it was so far back in time that the ladies who lived there still wore long skirts and bonnets. The married ladies wore white bonnets and the widows wore black ones. As children, we didn't really realise this was strange, we just saw it as 'what they did in Staithes.'

Back at the caravan, we got to know our neighbours and lots of them had children that we became friends with. They had never heard of West Bromwich, unless we mentioned West Bromwich Albion, and lots of people in West Bromwich hadn't heard of Bridlington. Being so small, when I was in Bridlington, they didn't understand my Black Country accent, and by the time we got home, I had developed a Yorkshire twang.

One family we became friendly with had the caravan next door to us. They lived in Hull and had two children. A boy and a girl. We had great fun with them and Christine and I had fabulous fun running around the caravan site making up games and playing happily together.

The man who owned the caravan site was a farmer, and as curmudgeonly as you like. Bad-tempered and he didn't like children. Not the best idea for someone with a caravan site.

We didn't have toilets in the caravans in those days, or running water. We used to have to fetch the water, and go down to the toilets. At night we had to run the gauntlet into the toilet block as the bobolas gathered around the lights to scare the living daylights out of us.

During the day, we would use the outside wall of the toilet block to play games and practice ball games up against it.

41

Every winter, the man who owned the camp-site would paint the toilets. One coat of gloss paint over another, it freshened it all up, but within no time, it would start to peel. As children, the sight of peeling paint was too much of a temptation and we would catch a little bit of paint and peel off as big a piece as we could. Often, the paint was so new, it hadn't really set properly so it made it even easier. We genuinely never realised what we were doing was wrong. It was just paint that peeled off and underneath was a different colour. One day, quite reasonably, it all got too much for him and he was heard screeching and complaining about his wrecked paintwork and demanded to know who had done it. We all denied all knowledge and he couldn't prove anything, but we never did it again.

There was a good group of children and in between visiting every castle, stately home, cove, and other piece of turf on the Yorkshire and Northumberland coast, we had fun on the caravan site.

Sometimes, we would travel from the caravan northwards and head off to Scotland. We got all the way to John-O-Groats, before we turned back.

Well actually, we didn't quite get to John-O-Groats. We got to the end of the road that leads to John-O-Groats, before Dad said, 'there's no point going the few extra miles just to say we have been there,' and promptly turned round and drove south. I was really disappointed, although thankfully he didn't say the same when we went to Land's End. We got to see some fabulous places, and we had some wonderful times.

Mum had an extraordinarily clever friend that she was at school with who was headmaster at Whitby Grammar school. We used to go and see them regularly and they had the most fabulous modern house. It was enormous. The hall had a dining table in it, big enough for a banquet, and enough rooms for everyone to have space to themselves. Granny had her own room and bathroom and up in the loft was the most amazing games room with the biggest train set you can imagine. Every boy's dream.

One day we were there and their children, a little bit older than my sister and me, took us outside to play. Ann taught me to ride a bike. I was so excited as I slowly learned to balance and then took off on my own. Turning and stopping came later, so every time I got to the end of the road, I had to put the brakes on and fall off slowly.

Their Dad was a genius. Dad was in awe of him and he always seemed to have his chair turned slightly away from us as he spoke. He was a lovely man, but a bit intimidating. They had enormous cheese plants that grew up and across the walls and every time we visited, we would look to see how much they had grown. He was very involved with the advent of the North Yorkshire Railway project, and we watched with eagerness as 'Johnnie-Potter's' railway came to fruition.

We would often visit Whitby for a day out and Mum, Chris and I would wander around the shops admiring the Whitby jet. Mum eventually bought a pendant and wore it all the time.

Back in Bridlington, one day when I was very small, we went to the beach. The sun was shining and we took all our buckets and spades, sandwiches and crisps, and Mum as ever took her knitting and a magazine, and off we went. Then I had a bit of an episode. I have no idea what happened, but I experienced, what I can only describe as a period of absence.

I got lost!

I remember nothing from before it happened, but all of a sudden, I 'woke up' and I was walking, crying and had a small shell in my hand which I had broken into small bits. I had no idea where I was and there was no sign of Mum and Dad. Out of nowhere two old ladies came to me and asked if I was lost. I nodded and they asked me which way I had come from. I had no idea, but pointed in a random direction, so they took me onto the lower promenade and we walked along.

Next thing I know, Dad is hurtling along and finds me. He thanked the two ladies for looking after me, then grabbed my hand, smacked the shell out of it and shouted at me for walking off. I cried and I remember vividly thinking, 'I feel like a teapot!' I felt like I was a shiny metal teapot and the inside was covered in tea stains, just like the one we used to use. I've no idea why I felt like that, but I'm sure the psychologists would have an answer. I realise now he must have been beside himself with worry, but it didn't feel like that to me then, I just felt I was in trouble. Back with Mum and Christine, I was reunited and told never to wander off again.

Often at the caravan, we used to spend time looking at the stars on clear nights. With very little light pollution, we could see so many and especially the Milky Way. Mum would point it out to us and it was simply wonderful. I don't know the names of many of the stars or constellations, but we would always look for the Plough, Orion's Belt and The North Star, then just stand and stare and watch as the others seem to come to life and light as if by magic.

One night there was a kerfuffle on the site and we discovered later, it was The Northern Lights, Aurora Borealis, which made people feel scared until we all discovered what it was. The dancing lights lit up the sky for a time and I distinctly remember a tree which looked like it was on fire, but not with real flames. I was totally hypnotised by the phenomena of it all and wanted to see it again.

Many years later, one evening at home with my husband, we saw the sky turn a neon, luminous green. We both thought some terrible explosion had happened or a pylon had been struck. It lasted about a minute and then disappeared. Then it all happened again. I spent a lot of time trying to find out what it was, and if any incidents had occurred, but nothing. I think we had briefly seen the Northern lights again.

As I write this, we are in 2022. It's been the most bizarre couple of years. We have so far survived a pandemic of Coronavirus, or Covid 19 as it's now known, and we have been once again counting our blessings for being here. Aside of all the traumas, there have been some lovely times too, and one of those for me was seeing the stars at night. They were so startlingly bright, with no pollution to mar the atmosphere, as there were no cars driving around, no aircraft, and the silence of it all was utterly wonderful. We were also truly blessed with the most amazing weather. We went into lockdown on my birthday. 23rd March 2020. The sun came out and shone upon us for months on end and unable to work, my husband Graham and I had a very special few months doing nothing in particular except for walking, cooking, eating, sitting in the garden and late night watching the stars.

I didn't realise how much I enjoyed looking at the stars until then, but found myself going outside every night and just staring at them. It reminded me of Bridlington as a child. The weather was so warm and the air smelt beautiful. With no people doing anything and no traffic noise it was just so incredibly peaceful, and we literally counted our lucky stars for being safe and sound.

Night Terrors

I've always dreamt a lot and I suffered with night terrors when I was a child. They were so distressing and regular, I wasn't allowed to sleep over at anyone's house until I was about 12 and the first time I did, was at my friend Carolyn's. Probably not the best place to start since the farmer who had lived there previously had shot apparently himself on the one landing and she showed me with suitable sadness where the bullet holes had been covered over. I used to run past it every time I went to the toilet.

My husband, Graham, will testify I still have traumatic dreams. Life in our bed is nothing if not unpredictable!

My dreams took on various recurrent themes. I do understand that they represented anxiety, but it made them no less vivid and disturbing. Over time, I am able to at least recognise often when I am having a nightmare and as I wake up feeling paralysed, with my heart pounding, I can now lie still and recover. I discovered fairly recently this is something referred to as sleep paralysis. When I was a child, it was a bit different.

There were several main dreams. The first was of a skeleton. I would wake up and at the side of my bed was a fully formed skeleton. Very white bones and his name was Fred. It's only recently that I have realised it was rather odd to have seen a fully formed skeleton. Every single bone was there. I have no idea where the image came from. Fred always had chips in his rib cage. They were chips from the chip shop. Not home-made. I would wake everyone up crying and screaming, and Dad would come and calm me down. Apparently, Mum couldn't calm me down, although it was Mum I always wanted. Eventually, I would calm down, wake up and go to the toilet. When I got there Fred was lying at the side of the toilet. In truth, there wasn't enough room for a skeleton at the side of the toilet, but he was there all the same. I would then wash my mouth with water. The inside of my mouth was very prickly, and in my mind, it felt like a hedgehog.

Every time I had a nightmare like this, next morning I would be asked by Dad, 'Do you remember what happened last night?'

Although it was probably a reasonable question, eventually, I used to say I couldn't remember. I didn't like the inquisition and hated feeling stared at.

The other three were probably less scary. I would wake up and see that the top third of the bedroom, above the pelmet, was on fire. Flames licked up to the ceiling all the way around. Over time, I realised the only way to put

45

the flames out was, in my mind's eye, to go and get the fire brigade and get them to hose it all down. Once the flames were out, I would be fine.

Another involved Mum travelling along the outside of a rectangle, whilst I travelled across the corner to corner. She was always wearing her mustard going-out dress. If we didn't arrive at the bottom right-hand corner together, I woke up having a nightmare. We never arrived together.

The next one, is one that has stayed with me in varied forms all my life and involves toilets! They always revolve around the toilets being unpleasant in some way. Dark, damp, old, overflowing, creepy, no doors, and all sorts of other problems that make using them inconvenient and unpleasant. Over the years I have managed to improve them by trying to educate my brain. Invariably it happens when I am anxious.

Another trauma I have when asleep is another typical out-of-control dream. These often involve me being in a car in which the handbrake doesn't work, rolling off the side of an edge, taking off over a bridge. Those started when I went flying with dad at the controls!

I also have dreams where I find myself falling asleep somewhere inappropriate, like driving, walking or working. I've learnt in the dream to recognise that I am asleep and try to close my eyes, which wakes me up, but it's still difficult! Lots of these dreams have their roots in things that have happened to me during my life and caused me anxiety.

Conversely, I have a couple of wonderful recurring dreams which always happen when I feel safe and happy, one involves horses, and another where I run so fast, I can fly. It has taken donkey's years, (pun intended,) to learn to fly in my dreams. Nowadays, I can fly quite easily and look around from above with no fear of falling.

No surprise about the horses as my young, fearless school-friend Carolyn, saved me from bullying. The flying is probably from the fact that I used to happily run everywhere when I was young. The more I could run the better, and sometimes I would think if I could run really fast, maybe I could fly.

46

Charlemont Primary School

I started infant's school at Easter. Dad took a photo of me on the lawn holding my pump bag next to our blackboard saying 'My First Day At School.' My sister had one done when she started school and I felt very proud.

I remember Mum taking me to school and holding my hand as we walked literally around the corner from our home to school. It was in the next street to ours. She gave me a kiss, and promised I could have steak and chips for dinner (now called lunch).

The morning went in a bit of a blur as we all sat in the first year's classroom with Mrs Hanby.

Later Mum came to fetch me and so the routine of school began.

One day, soon after I was at school, Mum and I went shopping. The shops were also very near, opposite the school and two minutes from home. As we walked to the shops, Mum told me how she really missed having my little hand to hold now I was at school. I was very upset feeling my mum was lonely without me.

In those days, 1968, Mum used to get all our groceries from the grocer's shop. Along with a butcher, greengrocer, (which also sold wet fish from time to time), newsagent, fish and chip shop, chemist, wool shop, hairdresser and most essentially, a sweet shop, our world of daily living was quite small. Everyone knew one another. Life was simple.

I enjoyed school and our class moved along year by year and eventually moved up to junior school. The infants and junior school were in the same building at either end and in the middle was the head teacher's office and secretaries. Charlemont primary consisted of one side of a 'U' shaped building. My godmother was one of the school secretaries and I felt very proud that she was 'My Godmother.'

One day, in infants' school, I remember, a few of us children were doing something very special and it meant we were in the school hall. Whilst the teacher was elsewhere, we were suddenly aware of being watched by a man outside who was crouched down and peering in at us through the double doors and big windows that ran along the one side.

He ran hunched up and although we weren't sure what it meant, we felt nervous. We told the teacher and all of a sudden, lots of teachers were running around in an agitated state. We were very gently asked to describe the man we had seen and assured we weren't in trouble and hadn't done anything wrong. We saw people rushing past outside looking for the man but I don't think they found him. I remembered only that he had sandy coloured hair. But we weren't allowed into the hall on our own afterwards.

I've no idea what happened afterwards, but as an adult, I can only imagine the fear and anxiety of what the teachers must have thought.

We had pump bags, for our PE equipment, and had to take a toilet bag for our toothbrushes so that we could clean our teeth at lunchtime. My toothbrush had Donald Duck on the end and I really liked it.

We had milk delivered every day and were given a bottle each with a straw. I loved milk. I still do, although it isn't very fashionable these days to admit to liking and drinking cow's milk.

In winter the milk was often frozen and we used to put it on the big heating pipes that ran around the edge of the classroom to give it time to melt by break time.

Every day we went into the hall for assembly. We would sit cross-legged, first years at the front and as we got older, we moved towards the back. We felt very grown-up when we finally reached the back row, and every day we were asked to show we had a clean handkerchief. We waved them cheerfully at the headmistress, before stuffing them back up our sleeves. Once a year, on our birthday, we were asked to stand up and everyone wished us happy birthday. Then we would be invited to go to see the head teacher who would give us an envelope with sweets in. We were so excited.

We had one wonderful primary teacher. Miss Worralo. She had a huge bosom, wore very short skirts and was so soft and kind. I remember she had a big pink cape and always left a trail of heady perfume in her wake.

I remember a Nigerian girl came to our school and we had never seen a black person before. Her palms were pink and I couldn't understand why she didn't just wash the rest of herself to wash the colour away. We became quite good friends and she came to some of my birthday parties. Eventually she left and I was amazed that people actually moved house.

I used to love the nature table. I liked it when we went for a walk and brought in leaves and flora to identify and although we all became very good at identifying the various leaves and which trees they came from, it's a skill I have, in the main, now lost.

I also used to love going to the zoo. It was an outing that took us by coach to Dudley Zoo now and again and seemed to take forever to get to. In fact, it was only a few miles away. On one such trip, David Harris and I managed somehow to get separated from the class and had the mickey taken out of us for ages afterwards as people speculated what we were up to. Once we were all together again, we went around looking at the various animals and eventually arrived at the ape enclosure. They were in a deep 'pit' area so we all looked down over the wall several feet above them. We threw them food including biscuits and a particular large Orang-Utan picked it up, chewed it thoroughly before taking it from his mouth, added in a handful of his warm and steaming pooh and flung it, with gusto, back up to the watching crowd. Too slow, Miss Worralo was covered in Orang-Utan poo and the force of it hitting her beautiful pink cape splattered several of us. We all found it very amusing although Miss Worralo was less impressed. I was especially proud to be at the zoo as 'My Godmother' accompanied us on the trip.

Back in the classroom, I remember learning the difference between would, could and should, there and their, to, too and two, where, wear and were, along with many other grammatical curiosities. We learned capital cities of countries, (I wasn't very good at those,) flags, (even worse), UK cities, (better), and that cities all had to have a cathedral. I was always good at spelling and still remember one day in junior school, the headmaster Mr Philips was taking our class and taught us how to spell Parliament. He told us it was easy to remember it as Par-lee-ay-ment. I've never forgotten how to spell it and still here his voice describing it so lyrically.

Speaking of which, one day we are told 'antidisestablishmentarianism is a very big word, if you can't spell it, you are the biggest dunce in the world. How do you spell it?'

Our pencils were on fire as we tried to work it out, and all groaned as the teacher explained the play on words and showed us, 'IT.'

Regularly, we would be given a big word on the blackboard and asked to make as many smaller words out of it as we could.

One day in primary school, we had a student teacher. She asked the class, 'Can we see the wind blowing?' I put my hand up and said 'No Miss.'

'Sorry, that's wrong' she said. Look outside the window, we can see the tree blowing and the leaves moving. We can see the wind.'

I was peeved, I put my hand up and said, 'Miss, we can see the tree moving but that isn't the wind, is it? The wind makes the tree move.'

Clearly no-one likes a smart arse, even though I wasn't trying to be, and she insisted the moving tree meant we can all see the wind. I'm not sure if she was just confused, misinformed or just daft, but I believed I was right and I used to sit looking out of the window for months trying to work out if I was right and wondering what the wind looked like. I believed I could only see the effect of the wind. Clearly, I've never quite forgiven her!

Another thing I have remembered all my life is one of our teachers telling us about spring. She said that the first snowdrops we see mean spring is

49

on its way. She said the snowdrops are the first flowers to bloom and although I was confused by crocuses appearing before them sometimes, I always am happy to see them and remember her words. She also lamented about how she loved to wake up in the morning and listen to the dawn chorus of the birds outside her bedroom window. I was very confused at this. She didn't explain exactly what the dawn chorus was and I wondered, did they line up on her windowsill and sing a song? How did they know the tune? I had never heard the dawn chorus, and wanted to wake early to hear one. I never did though.

Once a year, Mr Whittle used to bring us his animals and we used to sit agog in the hall as he got all his animals out to show us. He had a beautiful owl and showed us that although they can spin their heads a long way, they don't actually spin around completely. We were keen to impart this to people who tried to tell us owls could spin their head around 360 degrees! He brought snakes, let us touch them and then draped a big boa constrictor around our necks. Those of us brave enough to touch the snakes were surprised at how warm they were and how slimy they weren't! My favourite animal was a chinchilla because it was so soft and furry.

What a shame he didn't bring house spiders, because I am still scared of them! He did bring a tarantula but we weren't allowed to hold it as we were told if we dropped it, it would break and die. I wasn't too worried about the tarantula as we didn't get them at home, and also, they were quite attractive being so furry.

Which brings me to my fear of spiders. Both my sister and I were afraid of spiders and other creepy crawlies, like earwigs, but spiders were the worst, and I'm afraid I have to put a big portion of blame for this onto my Dad. I'm convinced he didn't like them either, but with his sometimes perverse sense of humour, after we had summoned him to catch the creepy crawly, he would then think it was really good fun to chase us with it in a tissue, and dangle it over our heads as we cowered behind the settee. If Mum was around, she would tell him off, but it was too late. With the odd creature dropping out of his hand, both my sister and I grew up with an understandable, irrational fear of spiders. Although this has got better as I've got older, I still rely on my husband Graham to deal with any stray creatures that come into the house.

When we were in our late 20's and both lived alone, I had, by now, learnt how to tackle spiders single-handedly. One night my phone rung. It was Christine and she was completely hysterical. It took a while to work out what was the matter and it turned out to be a spider. She was trapped on the stairs and a big spider was between her and the hoover.

After a few minutes, she eventually calmed down enough to be brave enough to go and get the hoover. Switching it on, she screamed loudly as she closed her eyes and waved the hoover wand over in the direction of the spider and eventually heard it rattle up the tube. She then went and poured herself a large brandy to calm her tattered nerves.

Meantime, back at primary school, we were learning how Hannibal led his elephants over the mountains. I was very worried about his feet as the teacher told us it was so cold and they didn't have special clothing or proper shoes and wore sandals. I couldn't imagine walking for days over mountains in a pair of sandals.

Once a year we used to walk across the playground into the other half of the school that adjoined us and into the big hall, where we mixed with the 'Holly Bugs.' These were the children from Hollyhedge Primary School. We were rivals of course and although the whole school building that we all shared, formed a big 'U shape, we had an invisible line in the playground between us that we never crossed! We were treated to an afternoon of cartoons brought to us by a man with a big projector and we all had a jolly good time.

At Christmas we used to have a nativity where most of us played a sheep or an angel, and one of my favourite lessons was when we used to make lanterns out of black paper and coloured acetate. I really liked doing this and I thought they looked like stained glass.

As young children, we went to each other's birthday parties, with sandwiches, cakes and jellies, played lots of lovely games. We also had a party in school once a year, where our mothers would send us into school with some food to donate to the party and we used to push back the tables and chairs to the walls of the classroom and play games. Mum always made a big red jelly and put it in her best glass bowl. I was very proud of it as everyone loved jelly.

We also used to have a day which was at the end of the school year, where we were allowed to take some toys in to play with. The whole day was full of fun and we played games like musical chairs with plenty of time to share and play with our toys and games.

At playtime we used to tumble out into the playground where we let off steam and played things like marlies, (marbles) which, as we got older included such additions as steelies, (ball bearings) and large marbles called something I can't quite recall.

We had skipping ropes and sometimes had a very large rope during PE where we learned to run in and out without tripping and sung songs to go with them.

'Cowboy Joe, lived in Mexico, hands up, pick 'em up, drop your guns and stick 'em up and out, you, go... Next person enters the rope and off we go again.

Another playground game was 'The farmer wants a wife,' where we all sat around in a circle and sung a song as someone who was picked to be a farmer skipped around the outside of the circle and at the appropriate time, picked a wife, then the wife wants a child, (she picked a child) the child wants dog, (the child picked a dog,) the dog wants a bone, and so on. We all wanted to be picked.

A game we sat in a circle for was 'I sent a letter to my love and on the way, I dropped it, somebody must have picked it up and put it in their pocket,' as someone would go around the outside of the circle with a letter and drop it behind someone. Both then had to run as fast as they can around the circle to see who could be first sit back down again.

Christine

I was very proud that my sister Chris, who was in the last year of juniors during my first, was one of the 'old ones' in the school. One day, we were all in the playground and we were having a race. It was a race that I was determined to win to show my sister how good I was.

The playground seemed really big, but it got smaller and smaller as a group of us raced from one side to the other to win by being first to touch the wall. We were neck and neck as we got towards the line, and the only way for me to win was to hit my brakes last. As everyone inevitably slowed down just as we got to the wall, I didn't.

Crash! I won! I hit the wall full pelt and smashed into it. I managed to turn away from it so avoided damaging my face, but my feet and legs weren't so lucky and I was bleeding. Chris took me to a teacher to get me patched up but at least I had won and she was pretty impressed. In fact, it seemed I had made an impression in all senses!

Another episode of my running full pelt took me from home around the corner and into the next road where the school was. Opposite school lived a friend of Mum who she met in hospital when she gave birth to Christine. Each Monday the two ladies would meet at alternate houses to chat and knit together. At the end of school, Christine, Jane, and I would go to whichever house we were at and we were given either a packet of fruit gums or a packet of fruit pastilles each. Then we children would play together, have tea together and then go home.

One day, I was running as fast as I could from home to Jane's and I turned around as I thought someone had called me. Unfortunately, I didn't stop running and failed to see the cast iron lamppost until it was too late.

Crash, although more of a 'Clang' sort of noise as I hit it full on. It's the one time I can say with absolute certainty that I saw stars and birds tweeting around the top of my head, just like a cartoon, and I was completely dazed.

Another time, Chris, Jane and I were walking along to Jane's house and a very fashionably-dressed young lady was walking towards us on the other side of the road. She had a very short skirt on, high heeled shoes and hair piled on top of her head in a big bouffant. Chris wasn't impressed and said she was very swanky. As we got closer to her, Chris shouted across to her, 'Wowee! What a whopper!.'

The lady wasn't happy! She strode over to us and bent down into Chris's face and said, 'If you ever say anything like that again, I'll rip your bloody swine out!'

We didn't know what a swine was and I remember talking about it and whether we all had one, although we didn't want to test it out! Lesson learned for now.

It's fair to say, Chris wasn't always overwhelmed with having a baby sister, and often wanted to send me back from whence I came! She was mischievous and often tried to get me into trouble.

One episode, which she will admit to, was putting lemon curd into Dad's custard. On Sundays we would have a pudding after our roast dinner, and invariably we would have custard with it, although Chris like Ambrosia Creamed Rice, so usually had that instead. Dad started to find Lemon Curd in his custard which he clearly didn't enjoy. Asking how it got there, Chris said it was me. I protested but got into trouble and told not to do it again. Unfortunately, it continued, and I was continuing to get the blame. Mum and Dad started to smell a rat, and out of sight, spied on Chris in the kitchen and saw her do it. When asked how it got there, she blamed me again and got the full force of Dad's ire! She was sent to bed for the rest of the day with no tea!

She was also known to have a bit of a temper, and as a small girl, would get so angry if something upset her, she would pick up the corner of the carpet and bite it as hard as she could. Dad called her 'little Hitler!'

As she got older, she decided to go to the Guides, after several weeks, mum needed to buy her a uniform. It was quite an expense, so she made sure Chris really wanted to join and we went over to Harborne to a shop that sold all the uniforms. All was going well, and Chris swore her allegiance to the Queen and seemed to really enjoy it. Then, out of the blue, she stopped going. She made some excuses but eventually it was obvious she didn't want to go anymore. Mum wasn't happy, having spent a lot on the uniform. Mum never really found out why Chris stopped going, but apparently it was because she got into trouble for playing with the boys in the Boys Brigade and was eventually expelled from guides for bad behaviour!

I often followed Chris in things, she being 2½ years older, although as we got older, if there was any challenge to our desire to do new things, she would regularly either just do her own thing quietly, without permission, or sometimes let me do the challenging and once sorted, follow in my footsteps.

She was always independent and would watch and wait rather than go in full throttle. We fell out as sisters do, but we were powerful allies when needs be.

Out of school, we often used to play in the street. There were lots of children about our age who lived in the street and we would play lots of games like French Cricket, British Bulldog, Hide and Seek, Tick, and any other games of the day.

There were only a couple of problems with this. One was a particularly grumpy policeman who used to tell us off for playing in the street and send us indoors if he saw us. The other was Granny-Gibbard. An old woman who lived in the care of her family and left her broom and pointy hat at the door. Woe-betide anyone who got caught as they crept onto the lawn to retrieve a stray ball. We all cowered and pulled straws to see who was going to be the one to run the gauntlet to get the ball. We did try being polite and knocked the door sometimes to ask if we could go onto the garden, but she was so scary and bad tempered, most of the time, we just ran, grabbed, and hoped we hadn't been seen.

As we were playing in the street one day, I stepped off the kerb and got run over by one of the neighbours' teenage sons who was riding his bike. My toe poured with blood and my toe nail grew with a big dent in it for years later. Although it wasn't his fault, he got the blame and was sent round to apologise for running me over with his careless cycling.

Meantime, in the classroom we were taught craft skills and artistic activities which seemed infinitely safer. I learned to do cross stitch, which I loved, I had learned to play the recorder so was able to play in the school band, and all in all life was happy.

Then the bully found me and it all became much less fun and nowhere near as safe.

Jess Maul

Understandably, I have changed the name of my bully. Her name doesn't really matter, her bullying did.

I don't know when or how it started, but at some point, I was sitting next to a girl who started to bully me. I have no idea why, but I'm sure the usual psychology factors of jealousy, envy, low self-esteem and other such explanations were the reasons. It really didn't make an ounce of difference to me as to why, I was only in primary school so only felt the effect of it. (A bit like the wind on the tree!)

She drew all over my exercise books, pulled my ponytail and constantly pulled out my elastic bobbles and broke them. Mum started to get cross and frustrated with how I managed to keep breaking them, but I was too scared to tell her. I don't know why I was scared of her or what I thought she was going to do to me but I kept quiet.

Jess made my life miserable. She decided that I was going to be her friend, whether I wanted to or not and invited herself to my house. Mum said it was ok and that she would make us tea. During the time Jess was at our house, she wanted to use the bathroom. She went upstairs and Mum went into a spin.

'Have you moved the towels?' she asked me.

Fear gripped me as I said, 'No, I forgot.'

Mum was irritated and Jess came back downstairs. Sensing some discord, she asked me what the matter was with my mum. I told her I was in trouble for not moving the towels. She was confused and I told her my Dad had brought them from work and would be in trouble if they found out. Oh dear, not my best reply.

You can guess what happened next. She threatened that if I didn't do as she said, she would 'spread that secret' and my Dad would go to prison. Revelling in her new found power, she then sat on my mum's favourite small wine table and broke it. Mum was really cross.

I had begged mum to crochet me a waistcoat, they were so fashionable at the time and so she spent hours crocheting it for me. Bright yellow as a base colour, like most things in the 60's it was a cacophony of all the gaudy colours of the spectrum. I was so thrilled with it and wore it to school. Jess was not happy, made me take it off and she wore it all day saying it was hers. She told me not to wear it to school again so I didn't. Mum was confused after I had badgered her into doing it, so I told her I wanted to keep it for best and wore it out of school and on holiday instead.

One day, Jess wanted me to go to her house after school and I couldn't think of a reason not to go. Mum had agreed, so off we went. Stopping at a sweet shop on the way, Jess disappeared from view for a moment and I took my opportunity to escape, ran out of the shop and all the way home. Mum was surprised to see me, and next day, Jess quizzed me as to where I had gone. I told her I lost her, couldn't find her so assumed she had gone on without me, so went back home.

As time went on, Jess also roped in her equally horrid cousin to help make me miserable, and although she was a bit older, so I didn't see her every day, she was still a huge pain in my side.

I am not sure how long the bullying went on for, but it seemed interminable and I remember thinking I must never make a mistake like letting on about a secret again. I felt that my life was ruined and I was forever blighted. However, in the end, it all got too much for me and I dissolved into tears in the classroom. I was sitting next to one of the boys who asked me what the matter was. I told him I had told Jess a secret and she was threatening to tell everyone. He promptly put his hand up and told the teacher. I think it was a student teacher, and her response was, 'Well, just don't tell her any secrets if you don't want people to know.' (She must have had a degree in hindsight), but at least it meant a few people in the class heard and one girl decided she would look after me.

Writing it makes it all seem so simple, but living through it day to day was one of the most miserable times I can remember. I hate any form of bullying and I've realised as I've got older, it's something that lots of people suffer both at school, work and home. Making someone feel isolated, threatened and imprisoned by fear, intimidation and shame is awful, and age, occupation and status make no difference to being bullied.

Carolyn

Carolyn was a breath of fresh air for me. She was confident and clever and had come to our school as we moved up into the Juniors, so about 8 years old.

She lived at the riding school that her mum owned and they had lots of horses. We became really good friends and she taught me to ride. Once she found out I was being bullied, she looked after me and effectively told them to 'get lost.' I felt a huge weight off my little shoulders. I was still scared of my Dad going to prison, and hated the sight of the towels in the bathroom, but peace returned and very slowly I regained my feeling of security and being happy and free again.

I loved the horses and Carolyn and I got on really well. She was a very strong and confident character and taught me so many things, lots of which have proved to be valuable lessons for all of my life. I developed a wide circle of friends and had lots of happy times.

As I grew older and became more accomplished at riding, I used to go to horse shows with her and sometimes got chance to take part in a gymkhana event. I also used to go to her pony parties which were a real joy and I was always very proud to receive 'proper' rosettes.

One day, after attending a gymkhana with Carolyn as her helper, we were sitting in the front of the Land Rover as her mum drove us home, all of a sudden, a big fat hairy spider came dangling down his thread just in front of my face. I screamed, her mum braked and the spider changed direction from swinging side to side, to back and forth. Landing on my head, I panicked and started jumping around, beating myself on the head. Carolyn and her mum thought it was really funny, but after I became slightly hysterical, eventually she pulled over and found the spider which was now in the foot well and removed him.

I learned all aspects of horse management as I helped out on the yard with the grooms, catching the horses, bringing them in, grooming, tacking up, cleaning the stables, feeding, and helping with new riders as we led them around, before turning them back out to pasture at the end of the day. Fairly often we were given a free ride as a reward and as I became even more accomplished would be given the responsibility of taking a newcomer out on a leading rein.

It's one of the few times in my life where I would happily and willingly get up early. One of the pleasures of this was riding the ponies to the yard after catching them in the morning and riding them again as we turned them back out.

Unfortunately, one day, one of the girls, around my age, fell off as she rode one of the pony's in, and landed badly on her elbow, smashing the bone quite badly and had to have surgery to fix it. Quite reasonably, we were then told we weren't allowed to ride the ponies bareback bringing them in and turning them out again. Of, course, after a week or two we soon started to ignore the rule and would walk them until we were out of sight and then remount to ride the rest of the way.

That was fine until one day, as we were turning them out and turned out of sight, we mounted the ponies. As we trotted along, the girl in front of me made me laugh. Her hair was bouncing up and down and I just found it hilarious. The more I laughed the funnier it became until eventually, I lost my balance and rolled off, right underneath the pony I was riding. Next thing I felt a hoof in the middle of my back as the pony trotted over me.

I wasn't sure how I felt, definitely winded, and my back felt odd. I lay there for a while unable to move. Eventually, I got the breath back in my lungs and went to get up. Everyone had stopped to help me. More than anything else, we were all frightened of getting into major trouble for riding when we shouldn't have been. My back felt bruised, but once I had got myself moving, I seemed to be ok. I was a bit worried I may have done something terrible and could only think that I would be in trouble for it, it. Fortunately, it seemed I hadn't suffered any catastrophic injury and I recovered. Being young I expect my bones were much more springy, especially as the pony was trotting.

Carolyn and I became really good friends and though it's hard to imagine these days, I was quite shy and loved that she was very self-assured and confident. I lived in the next street to school so she would regularly come for lunch at my house when we were at school and share fish fingers and chips or whatever else mum had cooked for us. I never stayed for school dinner as it was so close to home.

As we got older and we moved to senior school, her mum would regularly pick us up and on the way home she would stop at the local shops and buy us an ice cream. Carolyn would almost always have a Lord Toffingham, choc-ice lolly and I generally had the same.

As time went by, I used to see her more and more and was often invited to stay the night. I was always disallowed to stay over due to my regular night terrors and Dad was worried I would have one and they wouldn't know what to do with me. However, as I got older and the night terrors became less often, one night I was allowed to stay over. Her mum assured Dad that I would be fine and she wouldn't go into a melt-down if I had a nightmare so off I went to stay with Carolyn. This was my very first night staying out from home and away from mum and dad. I was really excited.

I went straight after school after being given a little overnight bag by Mum. Having never stayed at a friend's house before, I was very excited.

Spending the night in the big old farmhouse, which had lots of creaks and squeaks in it was a thrilling prospect. They had a wonderful Alsatian called Carlos who was a brilliant guard dog, but very gentle with us. His bark was deep and strong and we always felt very safe with him around.

Carolyn's bedroom was huge, and filled with all sorts of girly things. She was a big reader and was instrumental in encouraging me to read. The first book she gave me to read was on the day I went to stay with her. It was The Lion, The Witch and The Wardrobe, by C.S Lewis and I couldn't wait to read it.

Generally, I tended only to read comics as a child and I think it was probably because I was always on the go and never had time to sit down and read a book. That said, Mum would always encourage us to read and used to take us to the library every two weeks to change our books and we were especially encouraged to read on holiday. Mum was very keen on using language properly and often when we were at the caravan she would play word games with us, scrabble was a favourite but we also used to play a game with cards which had letters on them instead of numbers called Lexicon.

We then had to decide on what we were going to eat that evening. I was a fussy eater as a child, I liked plain food and didn't have a big appetite. I think I was far too busy running around to be bothered with food. Carolyn suggested we get a take-away, which was something I'd never experienced and next thing we were driving to collect our food. It was something called 'Kentucky Fried Chicken.' made by a man called Colonel Sanders and came in a box. It was the first time I'd ever heard of it and was amazed at the experience. Arriving home, we ate it with our fingers and it was quite spicy. Being in a different environment I really enjoyed it.

We spent a very happy evening together and then it was time for bed. As it was a special night Carolyn said we could have a midnight feast, which felt very exciting. We went to bed and our feast food was something else I'd never tried called a 'Pot Noodle.' I'd heard of it but had never eaten one.

It was amazing. We boiled the kettle poured on water, left it for 5 minutes and voila, we had food in a pot! I remember it was chicken and mushroom and I was amazed how lovely it was having seen the dried-out version just a few minutes earlier. I can still remember the taste of it being quite salty but liking the texture of the noodles which was something else I'd never eaten before. I didn't even know what noodles were let alone know how to eat them. Carolyn showed me how to twirl it round a fork and get it into my mouth before it all dropped off. I don't think I've ever had one since so am left with a rosy-tinted view of my first and last 'Pot Noodle.'

We had an uneventful night and I slept soundly with no nasty nightmares. It set the scene for me being allowed to stay over with her now and again more easily, and I never had any nightmares.

Once I'd read the book, she leant me the rest of the series and I really enjoyed them and I was then introduced to 'The Mallory Towers' series of books which I loved, and was so disappointed when I got to the end of them. Horsey books were a must as you would expect and I would immerse myself wishing it was me in the books. On TV, we had the adventures of 'Black Beauty,' 'Follyfoot' and we had another series called 'White Horses,' which was a foreign series, and dubbed, but we all loved it and especially the song that started and ended the programme.

I learnt so many things from being with Carolyn and her Mum and working with horses. Many have stayed with me all my life and have served me well especially in times of crisis.

One of the first lessons was about holding the reins. I distinctly remember Carolyn's mum teaching me that horses have a very sensitive mouth. Because their mouth is so soft, holding the reins which are attached to the bit means they can detect any sort of nervousness that passes from your hands to the reins. I took this very literally and from then on, no matter how nervous I might have felt, I made as sure as I could, that none of my nervousness would show to the horse. I kept my breathing under control and tried to relax my body to ensure the reins didn't tighten or shake in my hands. Panic on a horse and it will take off like a rocket with you atop. Animals are very attuned to the nuances of danger and when you are sitting on a horse, you have to hang on for grim life or else risk being thrown off in an inelegant heap. Horses have a brilliant set of brakes that don't extent to the person on the top!

Using the same principal of the reins, keeping calm in a crisis is something I have done countless times in my life in response to fear or anxiety. I try to keep a cool air and use my head rather than panic. It has served me well it is rare that I ever panic.

Another lesson I learned was all about body language and psychology, and it is of course the same to our fellow humans. Smiling, open gestures, being authoritative but not aggressive makes horses, as well as humans, feel safe.

We refer to horse analogies all the time. 'As stubborn as a mule.' 'Lead a horse to water but you can't make it drink it,' and keeping something on a tight rein are sayings we are all familiar with and very true. Horses like to know their place and with us humans to lead them they will generally acquiesce. I learnt to gently breathe up their nose to make friends and was surprised how they would breathe back.

Bearing in mind I am now a colonic hydrotherapist and digestive specialist, it won't come as a surprise that I learnt a lot about the gut from working with horses. They are designed to eat scrub land and graze all day in order to get enough nutrients. Put them onto a rich grass diet or too much high energy food and they suffer. Lameness sets in or they develop colic which for horses was almost always a very traumatic killer. They would suffer a twisted gut and it would be rare that they would recover. We learnt never to ride a horse after being fed a meal or after drinking lots of water. When they are hot, they need to cool down slowly, not be given a big drink. They needed to be fed to their needs not just because we want to feed them for love.

Nowadays, I regularly use horses as an example of how we humans should look after our own digestive health. I have never been able to exercise on a full stomach. I always needed at least 2-3 hours after food before I could even think about doing a gym workout. Everyone is slightly different but I'm sure you certainly can relate to not being able to exercise after having a big meal and how eating makes us sleepy afterwards. Rest and digest is the key.

I spent many happy years with Carolyn, her mum and their horses and I am ever grateful for all the lessons I learnt from all of them.

One summer, Carolyn's mum gave me and another girl a task of bringing on two ponies who needed time and effort to get them ready for riding. One was springy and bouncy, the other was stubborn and lazy. I had the one that was stubborn and lazy and although he had the most wonderful temperament, getting him to move was a hard job. He wouldn't go in front of any other horse and would only follow. It was a difficult job to get him to go anywhere on his own but eventually he got better at it and we saw a big improvement. He was never going to be a racehorse but his confidence improved dramatically and so did mine. I could see the difference my efforts made to him and it gave me great pleasure. It was wonderful to be able to ride him almost whenever I wanted to and one day, he found a new home with a lovely family who bought him for their 2 children. I still have a photo of me riding him at one of the riding school shows and he looked very splendid with plaited mane and tail, another skill I was taught!

As we got older, the pony parties were replaced with house parties and the first time I ever went to a night club was to celebrate Carolyn's 18th birthday. We had VIP tickets to a night club in Birmingham city centre. We had a lovely evening and didn't get back until the early hours. I'd never been out so late into the night!

At one of her house parties when we were younger, I was dropped off with two friends. Sally and another girl. I'll call her Melody. Her mum and dad lived in a big house near us and they had a huge garden. She had the prettiest bedroom I had ever seen and she had a vanity case, something I coveted with its solid box shape and little pots for creams and potions. I knew her from the first day of school and we were firm friends. She suffered asthma and eczema so didn't tend to join the rough and tumble of our games and didn't ride horses. But she was a gentle, lovely girl and came to Carolyn's party on this occasion. Her Dad wasn't very tall and drove a big car. On the night of this particular party, he had agreed to pick the three of us up. Around the time he was due, we were waiting in the hall. Music was playing and people were chatting so the noise level was quite high, we thought we heard the door-bell ring and the four of us all looked at the front door which had a diamond shaped, bull-nose pane of glass. We couldn't see anyone

Someone said, 'Is there someone at the door?'

I replied, 'It must be Melody's Dad as there's no-one there!'

Fortunately, Melody didn't hear what I said, but the three of us were giggling and she looked a bit confused. Next thing, the door-bell rings again and there's still no sign of anyone. Carolyn went to open the door and Melody's Dad was standing there! Although I had said it in jest, I had been right and we burst out laughing. Melody was asking us what the joke was and we made something up, but I don't think she was convinced. Sitting in the back of the car, which was huge, we couldn't see Melody's Dad and Sally and I giggled all the way home as it looked for all the world that the car was driving itself.

Piano Playing

Dad was regularly invited to play piano at the MEB social club which he did from time to time. Mum and Dad didn't go to social clubs or the like, but as children, every year around November, Dad would join the social club as a member. He did it because everyone who was a social club member and had children, were given Christmas presents for the children up to the age of 14. Dad saw an opportunity and would join for a few weeks and then leave in January. For as long as the presents were more value and pleasing than the cost of the membership, Dad continued! At the age of around 16, Dad having extended our birthdays somewhat to say we were still 14 and under, he felt he had pushed it as far as possible and we received our last gifts. We were all glad as we had rather outgrown the gifts which were based on age, although during the years before some of them were really lovely!

Both mum and dad played piano, and both had had lessons when they were younger and passed exams. One day, they asked us if we would like a piano and sometime later it arrived. I remember it vividly as the piano was carefully brought in through the front door on a wooden trolley and after rearranging the lounge furniture, the piano was installed. It was a 'Mignon,' which took a while to learn how to pronounce. It was highly polished dark wood and very beautiful. Very soon dad was playing and really enjoying it. He played modern music mainly. Mrs Mills, Russ Conway and honky-tonk style music. Mum stuck generally to classical music and always read the music rather than play by memory. She would be irritated if she got her fingers tangled up and hit the wrong keys.

Dad decided Chris and I should learn to play piano too. Like most children, we had played the recorder at school, and I had played the bass and treble recorder, my highlight was being able to play at West Bromwich Town Hall when I was still at Charlemont Primary School, playing for several nights of 'Joseph and the Amazing Technicolour Dreamcoat.' It was a very new production then being written in the late 1960's, and I found the whole event overwhelmingly beautiful, with the production, delightful songs and choral singing. All the schools in West Bromwich borough were invited to collaborate and contribute a number of children for the choir, orchestra and acting. Mum made me a new long black skirt and we performed for 3 nights. It was a wonderful privilege and we felt we were far better than any future West End stage production could perform!

I started playing the piano by trial and error, picking out tunes from memory and finding the right notes to play a simple tune. I enjoyed it. Dad then started to teach us the basics of the piano musical notes and scales.

I was quite good at reading music, and enjoyed learning scales to begin with, learning which fingers played which notes, how to hold the correct posture of wrists and fingers, crossing them over properly, it was all very interesting. Starting with middle 'C,' I soon got the hang of the notes.

Then we progressed to the bass notes, left hand and it was all going rather well. We had a music book with lots of tunes in it and I enjoyed playing things like, 'Ode to Joy,' 'Morning has Broken,' and eventually progressing to a bigger, but older music book with buff-coloured pages and playing 'Fur Elise.'

Inevitably, the novelty wore off a bit, and rather than encouraging us to let us play as and when we felt the desire, Dad decided we had to practice! Big mistake I think, as it turned something that was previously pleasurable and fun, into a huge chore of, 'Have you done your 15 minutes of piano practice?' every day!

We had another few traumas as the battle of wills swung between Dad wanting us to practice piano every day, and Chris and I not wanting to! Chris wasn't as musical as I was in any case, and inevitably it went downhill and we eventually gave up playing. I would sometimes go and play, especially if dad was out, as if he heard me play, he would start asking me to practice again. Eventually he gave up and I played now and again, but never really took it up properly.

I asked Chris about her memory of the piano and she said she just deliberately made a hash of it so that Dad wouldn't nag her to play! It must have worked because I can hardly ever remember Chris sitting at the piano.

Back in School

During our last year at junior school, the Government encouraged us all to start to go green and look after the environment. It was 1973 and 'Plant a tree year.' We felt very important as we walked down to Charlemont Farm Estate to 'Plant a tree in '73.' The following year, we were all asked to 'Plant some more in '74.' I haven't been to see if our trees have survived, but, (as I write,) they will now all be around 50 something years old. We then had the 'Keep Britain Tidy' campaign where it seemed, all the bins had the logo on them. The country was changing.

We also had a new precinct. West Bromwich High Street changed forever as the 'Queen's Square' emerged closely followed by the 'Kings Square.' We could do all our shopping under cover and it all felt very modern. There were two big supermarkets, and generally people either chose Tesco or Sainsbury's to shop, but rarely did they go to both!

One student teacher in primary school encouraged us to sew and do embroidery and along with others, Carolyn and I each made a big fabric collage. Mine followed me around for years, and every time there was an art competition at senior school, I entered it and did well! In the end it became so tattered and battered, I had to let it go.

Our last student teacher had a lovely, lilting Yorkshire twang and read us a new book that had been issued called 'Stig Of The Dump.' I can still here her saying 'Bu' Steeg' as she read animatedly to us all.

Towards the end of junior school, we were introduced into the world of 'Richardson writing' Until this time, I don't believe my writing as a child was any better or worse than any of my school friends. Thanks to the wondrous invention by Mrs Richardson, this was about to change.

It was apparently supposed to make joined-up writing easier as it had a series of wide loops and open circles. Although a few people seemed to do well with it, most didn't and I was one of them. What happened was that it served to confuse my brain so much that my writing became appalling and has remained so ever since. On the basis of my writing, I would have been a brilliant doctor!

Dad had difficulty writing too, apart from his dyslexia, he couldn't hold a pen and complained as he got older that holding a pen and trying to write was almost impossible as his hand, wrist and arm hurt and he couldn't control the pen. He couldn't write more than a few lines without his arm hurting and his writing was poor. As I have got older, I have seemingly inherited the same problem. I can't hold a pen properly, struggle to write more than a couple of lines and often the pen will fly out of my hand. No-one can read my writing, including me, and no matter how hard I try, I can't do it. It feels as though I can't control the strength of how tightly I hold the pen, or how I move it across the page. Thankfully, computers and I-pads now take the strain, and my husband writes most of our cards or envelopes although I would still love to be able to write properly.

All too soon, we were in our final year of primary school. During our years we had learned to spell, count, stand in straight lines and sit up straight at our desks. The school nurse had pulled our hair searching for nits and checked our feet at regular intervals for warts, verrucae and other miscellaneous complaints. The visiting dentist had checked our teeth for signs of decay, and in PE we had all learned 'Movement to music,' which most of us hated. 'Let's all be an elephant,' or 'Now, be a tree,' as we all stood straight with our arms waving about like trunks or branches, as the voice told us and the screechy music rung in our ears. None of us really got the point of it, but seemingly we were now perfectly prepared for the big move to senior school.

So, as the summer came and went, and senior school loomed large we were all excited and a bit scared as we were put into 'House' groups. I was to be a Trojan, the same as my sister and coincidentally, the same as my mum had been when Menzies was a grammar school. I was once again proud to follow my sister.

Menzies

Luckily, I had just missed the dreaded 11 plus exams and so we were all off to Menzies High School. A relatively new comprehensive, and recently converted from grammar school.

The first day arrived and with it the obligatory photo with the blackboard entitled, 'My First day at Menzies.'

Armed with a satchel, which I was very proud to have been given from someone, and a brand-new sparkly uniform in my favourite colour of blue, off I went accompanied by another friend, Jackie. We arrived at school early, walked down the long slope and reached the top of a flight of steps that led down to the main area of the school.

Splat! I tripped and tumbled head first down the steps and into an embarrassing heap at the bottom. Struggling to regain my composure and hoping that the whole of the school hadn't seen me, I jumped up, straightened everything, and walked on. I remember vividly thinking, I hope this isn't a sign of things to come. Just as I had been given a beautiful, blank page for life ahead, and a new chapter dawned, it was already a bit dog-eared and damaged.

Recently, on a regular Facebook-banter exchange with one of my old teachers, now a friend, he was teasing me over my first day fall, and I commented that to fall flat on my face and get up laughing, was probably a great first lesson on the first day of senior school. Learning is just as important and valuable with the trips, slips and mistakes, as it is from getting everything right first time.

Finding our way to the large school hall, we are sorted into our House groups and led to our classroom. Every morning we have to meet here for registration with our House-Tutor. We are each given a timetable and everyone's is slightly different as we are also sorted into ability groups. Before we know it, we are walking from classroom to classroom for new lessons with new teachers and we soon start making new friends.

Most of the children from Hollyhedge joined us and before long we were a generally good cohesive group. There were a couple of people we would rather avoid, and for me I tried to keep away from any trouble. One experience of bullying was more than enough and although Jess was there, we were in different House groups and different lesson groups. I wonder if she ever gave me a second thought, and even more if she can even remember the misery she inflicted upon me now that we are nearly 60.

We had four 'Houses.' Trojan, Spartan, Olympian and Greek and for our year group, Spartan's won almost everything, especially sport. We Trojans didn't give up without a fight though and with some sterling performances along the way we did our best to give them a run for their money. We also had art and music competitions and there was a friendly rivalry between groups. Each house also had a colour. Red for Trojan, Yellow for Spartan, Green for Olympian, and Blue for Greek.

I loved sport and games and although terrible at throwing, I was enthusiastic and more than willing to partake in most things. I played for the school teams in netball, hockey, and more especially running. I also loved badminton and rounders but as always, I was hopeless at anything that involved a small object being aimed at me and an implement to hit it back with! 'Keep your eye on the ball,' (or shuttlecock) we were told. I did, I really, absolutely did, and watched it fly past me 99 times out of 100. Occasionally, I hit it back and that was a spectacular achievement. I am still hopeless at hitting small objects with a bat and I'm not any better at throwing or catching, but I am very enthusiastic!

As I have said, I grew up running. If I could run instead of walk, I would. My only reason was to get from A-B as quickly as possible. At primary school, this was more of a need as I left home as late as possible having been torn out of a warm bed into the cold day. (Nothing much has changed as I've got older.) I am still waiting for the day when I wake early and jump out of bed!

I didn't know how good I had become though, until the end of my first year at sports day. We were encouraged to enter events to represent our House group. We could do a maximum of two track and one field, or two field and one track event. I was quite good at the high jump, so did that, and I was entered into the 400m and 800m track event.

All of us that were competing were taken by coach to Hadley Stadium in Smethwick. Having never raced in my life, apart from into the wall at Charlemont, I just ran and ran, and next thing I had come second in the 400 metres and won the 800 metres. Christine, being 3 years ahead of me in school years, was watching from the stands and seemingly immensely proud of her little sister, and believe me, that hasn't happened too often!

A girl in Christine's year saw me run and asked Christine to see if I would like to go to train with her at Birchfield Harriers running club. I was very keen to go. Excitedly I asked Mum and she said yes, Dad however wasn't so keen.

I was extremely slim as a child. I suppose I would be called thin. I wasn't anorexic, I was just thin. I was so active I presume I just burnt it off, and I was perfectly healthy. The advice of the doctor all those years before to get lots of fresh air and get fit had paid off.

Dad wasn't interested in sport and I don't think he could really see the point of me wanting to go running. He put a real damper on it all and said I couldn't go because I was too thin and it would make me ill. I was really upset, so in the end Mum made an appointment for me to see the doctor to give me a check-up. The same doctor who I had seen all those years before said I was perfectly fine and fit, and recommended I go out in the fresh air and enjoy my running saying it would be good for my health and lungs. Reluctantly, Dad couldn't really refuse to let me go, although he never aided me in any way. I wasn't bothered. I got two buses there with Cathy and often her mum would pick us up at the end of training.

I really loved it. The first time I went, a trial was going on and people were being picked for a race. As we ran around and around the track, I realised I needed to slow down. I was in danger of being in the first few to finish. As time went on, I realised that although I loved the training, I didn't like the idea of competing. Everyone who was competing was expected to commit a lot more time to training and I didn't want to do that. So, I kept in the background as much as I could and did my training programme as it was. It always started with a 10 lap warm up and then lots of sprints, stretches and gym work afterwards.

Nowadays, I think I would probably have been quite a good long-distance runner. I wasn't built for speed, but I had an amazing amount of endurance. Now, although I have less of both, it's still more stamina than speed.

At the end of the first year at Menzies, I was completely surprised to receive my House colours. House colours were awarded for being outstanding in something. Mine was mainly for running although I think a lot of it was also for taking part. I was told it was the first time they had given it to someone in the first year, but I can't believe that so maybe it was just a bit rare. Either way, I was very excited and proud as I was handed a red ribbon to sew on my tie.

As time progressed, I represented the school and county running up to 1,500 metres. At one meeting I was running the 800 metres and wasn't feeling great. I finished but my time was very slow and when my geography teacher, John Parkes found out he regularly took the mickey out of me. Eventually, I said, 'well if you are so good, let's have a race!' Sports day was coming up and seemed the perfect opportunity to put our skills to the test. Needless to say, we never had our race, John citing all sorts of reasons, mainly that he had a leg injury, although it didn't stop him playing football! It became, and remains, a 'running joke!'

Today, I met my friend Deana for breakfast. I was telling her my book was ready for printing and she told me a story of when we used to do cross country running in the winter months. We would do a circuit of the extensive playing fields behind the school, which were also very muddy. We would end up filthy and definitely needed a shower afterwards. I loved it, as I loved all running, and jumping over puddles without breaking stride was fun. Deana told me she and another 3 girls used to divert off the run and go to Deana's nan's house nearby in Coles Crescent. Even though one day we were all called in early, which meant they arrived late, they never got found out. I had no idea they used to do this until she told me.

Like most people, some lessons were more pleasurable than others. Although we were all bored stiff by some of the lessons, one lesson was taught by Miss Hugget. She was a lovely lady and taught us R.E. Religious Education. Delightfully kind, she saw only good in everyone, she was very naïve and a bit of a target for us to play up. She didn't really help herself in her introduction of herself.

'My name is Miss Hugget, and the best way to remember my name is what you do with your Teddy bear... You Hugget!' We all tittered and giggled at the analogy.

The classrooms in some of the blocks had huge sliding glass windows and during one particular lesson one of the boys opened the window and climbed out while Miss Hugget had her back to the class. Running round the outside of the building, he then knocked on the classroom door, came in and apologised for being late. Apology accepted, he retook his place.

Inspired, someone else did the same thing and got the same response. He retook his place too. By the time the fifth or sixth person had done the same, Miss Hugget smelt a rat and for one of the few times in her teaching life, got really cross and shouted at us.

French was another lesson I didn't enjoy. I couldn't see the point of it, since the prospect of using it was never likely to happen. The idea of travelling to France or working there wasn't even on the radar. A lot of the boys enjoyed French, but mainly because we had a very lovely French teacher who they all found very attractive!

I enjoyed Needlework and Home Economics, in fact most of the practical subjects were more me. At the end of the year, we would have prize-giving and one person for each subject was rewarded with a book voucher for showing either aptitude or enthusiasm. I used to win the needlework prize, but I think it was mainly because no-one else really enjoyed it. Usefully one of our first lessons in needlework was to make an apron for home economics.

During Home Economics, we learned how to wash up properly and I remember having to write an essay on 'How to wash up' which involved leaving the greasiest dishes until last and not having the water too hot for the glasses in case they shattered. I also learned using a clean cloth and clean tea towel prevented bacteria being transferred but that the best way of drying dishes was to rinse them with hot clean water and leave them to drain naturally. Skills for life!

We also used to cook. Some weeks we were told what we were cooking, but sometimes we had a free week to cook whatever we wanted to. I almost always made a quiche on these occasions whilst other people were being really adventurous with devilled kidneys and boeuf bourguignon.

As a reminder of how many times I made a quiche, when I was 18, my friend Jackie bought me a flan dish. I've still got it, and I still make them.

Every year, twice a year, the fair came to town. Dartmouth Park in West Bromwich was, and still is, a lovely place and as children, on Sunday mornings, Dad would take Chris and me to the park to play on the swings and slides. Then we would go down to the boating lake and Dad, knowing the man who ran it, would invariably get us a free turn on the rowing boats. Dad was good at rowing and he taught both of us how to row. Giving us the finer points of skimming the oars across the top of the water, he would allow us to take it in turns to have a go. Chris was better at it than I was, but my defence is that I was so small, not only was I not able to reach the foot rest that you could lean against to pull the oars, neither could I really hold the weight of the heavy wooden oars. Sometimes if I was really struggling, I'd do one oar at a time and we would weave and wobble our way around the lake. Dad used to laugh as I tried to row a boat that was clearly too big for me and we would end up going round in a big circle.

We would then feed the ducks on the lake and go home to a lovely Sunday roast beef dinner that Mum had prepared while we were out.
As we got older, the park became the centre of West Bromwich events and when we were at Menzies, in November, as bonfire night arrived, so did the fair. We used to get really excited as we met up to walk to the park.

Wrapped up against the cold, we would go on a few of the rides. I liked some of them, but hated others with a passion. I was fine as long as they were on the ground so the 'Waltzers' and 'Cyclone' were great, but anything that went in the air and also spun around in the air was an absolute no-no. One year we were at the fair and at the bottom of the 'Octopus' ride. I was refusing to go on as I was scared, and the girls were going on at me to have a go. Eventually, one of the girls said 'Gill, come on with me and I promise I won't ask them to spin us.' Unwisely I agreed.

It wasn't a happy experience. Even without the man spinning us round, the car was spinning around on its own. It soared up and down and round and round as I gripped the hand bar with true white knuckles, screaming my head off and trying not to panic. The girl who was with me was petrified of my reaction and also ended up in a traumatic state. At the end of the ride, we got off and she said to the other girls, don't ever ask Gill to go on anything like that again. She doesn't like it!

One day at the fair, we played on the 'Hook-a-duck' stall and I won a goldfish. Taking him home in a plastic bag, he was my one and only pet. Mum looked after him as he swum around a Pyrex bowl and he lived in the hall on top of the wooden tea trolley for a number of years. Mum decided one day to put some gravel in the bottom of the bowl to make his life a bit more interesting. Unfortunately, he swallowed a bit of gravel and got it trapped in his mouth. As he swam around the bowl, every time he hit the side, he set off a gentle ringing noise. Mum decided to help him and after holding him under a running tap, managed to get a thick needle into his mouth and eventually flick out the offending bit of gravel. He was returned to a gravel-less bowl and lived a happy life going round and round watching us all go by.

Christine decided she wanted a fish too so we went and won another one. She called him Fred and he lived in a similar Pyrex bowl upstairs on a wooden blanket box. He had a tendency to escape and regularly jumped out. One day, he jumped out and disappeared. We looked everywhere but he couldn't be found. 24 hours later and Mum was upstairs and heard a thudding sound, eventually she found Fred, stiff as a board and covered in fluff behind the blanket box, but amazingly still alive. She popped him back in his bowl and poked him a bit, dropped a bit of brandy in the water and amazingly he survived. He went on to live for several years afterwards too!

My Godfather was a journalist. He worked for several newspapers during his career and had a reputation for making a story out of nothing. One day Mum was telling him about our fish and the following week we read all about it in the West Bromwich Chronicle. 'A Tale of Two Fishes,' we were so proud to be in print.

Another thing we were regularly in print for was for collecting milk bottle tops. In those days, all milk came in a bottle with a foil lid. We washed them, and collected them all and eventually, we would have enough to donate to the 'Guide Dogs for the Blind.' They would reward us by publishing our names in the newspaper and give us thanks. At Christmas time we would also collect used stamps and those would be collected too.

In our world of waste not, want not, any post that was delivered with an unfranked stamp, was soaked in water, removed, dried and reused with a bit of glue. This evolved for a time into rubbing off the frank mark if it wasn't too deep and reusing those stamps too. Luckily, the Queen didn't find out as I'm sure she would have had us thrown in the tower for treason, and fortunately the Royal Mail survived a few dodgy stamps.

Mum and Dad had some friends who lived in a beautiful house in Walsall. They had a son around our age and we always had a good time there. He was also an electrician so Dad was in his element talking to him. Going through the hall, the lounge led off it, through double doors and it always seemed very grand. We used to play with their son and our favourite game was sliding down the stairs on their carpet! There was a gentle bend on their stairs so it meant we had to guide our way around it to avoid crashing into the wall, and for some reason, we seemed to be able to build up a good speed as we did it.

This may sound an odd game, but sliding down the stairs head first was fun and we weren't allowed to do it at home because Mum and Dad said it pulled the carpet off the treads. Our carpet was a strip that went down the middle and held in place by stair-rod grips so not as secure as the lovely fully fitted carpet the 'Preedy's' had. Either way, we had lots of fun probably because it was a rare treat for us having an impromptu slide.

Dad's father, we called Bampa, was a kindly man, also an electrician, and died of a brain haemorrhage aged just 66. He always seemed to be smiling. I was only young when he died but I remember him well. He always seemed to be wearing a grey knitted cardigan and was rotund. He used to make a slide for us in their garden out of a gym bench, (no idea where that came from!) and although it was fun, the rubber stops at the bottom could inflict a nasty bump and bruise if we misjudged it and of course it was very short so not as good as the Preedy's stairs!

One evening we went out and Mum and Dad said we were going to The Preedy's! Chris and I were happy. As we got to their house, Dad drove straight past. As he continued to where he could turn around, he said, 'Oh look, a circus! You like circuses don't you, would you like to go?'

Before I could say yes, Chris said, 'No! I hate them!'

Which was a shame, because unbeknown to us, that's where we were going! They had hoped to give us a lovely surprise, but clearly Chris wasn't amused. I was much happier. I liked the Circus. We sometimes used to go when we were in Bridlington to 'Billy Smart's' circus, and others that came occasionally. Unperturbed, we arrived at the big top at Walsall Arboretum and took our seats high up in the tent.

It was a cold night and we had our anoraks on to help keep us warm. Whilst Dad and I enjoyed it, Chris put up with it, although I think she enjoyed some of the acts in the end. Mum however, was completely distracted by a man who happened to sit next to her and was struggling with the zip to his coat. The fabric had become trapped in the zip and he couldn't shift it. Mum offered to help and spent most of the evening fighting to release it all for him. He couldn't take his coat off as it was stuck half way up and not enough space to wrestle it off. Eventually with much tugging and pulling, she did it, but had missed most of the show!

David Harris Reads English.

David Harris and I were good friends. We spent time playing together as children in primary school. I don't remember why or how we became friends and he can't remember the events as well as I do, but having described where we used to play in the huge loft space above the garage at his parents' home, it's clear that I was there at various times. I remember his mum was an especially lovely lady. We were in the same class at primary school all the way through until we moved to senior school.

Mr Gale was one of our English teachers. Slightly eccentric and easily distracted, he would tell us lots of tales about his diving expeditions. He held a wonderful world record for 'The longest underground swim under a tunnel,' which was in the Guinness Book of Records for many years, mainly because the said tunnel was later closed so it couldn't be equalled.

He also regularly used to go diving in a big pool on the playing fields behind the school, which always looked miserable cold and murky. We had no idea what there could possibly be in there to find interesting.

There were several incidents in his English classes, but one which gave me the most humiliation was from David Harris. We had been in the same class since infant's school and he used to play me up whenever possible. Always good humoured but it was an ongoing event.

One day in English, we were given a 'free choice' of what to write an essay about. A week later, in class, Mr Gale asked, 'Who wants to read out their story?'

David's hand shot up. Unusual really as none of us were very keen to share our literary skills with our classmates.

'Thank you David. Please read your story.' Said Mr Gale.

David stood up and proceeded to read.

'Last week, me and some of my friends were coming back from the boys club and walked back along Thursfield Road.' My ears pricked up and I had a bad feeling about what was coming next.

'As we got to Gillian Skidmore's house, we knocked the door and ran off for a joke. As we ran away, Gillian Skidmore's Dad chased us on Gillian Skidmore's bike and he had a crow bar in his hand which he threw at us. He chased us to the new houses where we hid and we waited for him to go.

I was right to have a bad feeling! Everyone in the class gasped and then laughed at what my Dad had done. I was so embarrassed and David had the biggest grin on his face having exacted revenge for what my Dad had done to him and his friends!

'Did your Dad really chase them with a crow bar?' people were asking.

'Unfortunately, yes,'
'And was he really riding your bike?'
'Unfortunately, yes.'
'Wow! How embarrassing for you!'
'Unfortunately, yes!'

For me I'm not sure which was worse, the knowledge that my Dad had acted in such an outrageously over the top, wild fashion, or the fact that he did it on my bike. Although it was a racing bike, it was still pink and girly and he looked absolutely ridiculous on it.

Dad didn't take kindly to childhood antics, which was a bit surprising really when he told us of some of the things he got up to when he was young. He told us tales of when he and his friends would tie letter boxes together along a whole street with a long piece of string and they would then knock one of the doors. Apparently, as the door was opened it set off the next one and resulted in all the residents coming to their door at the same time and set off each other's door knockers along the street! Smacks of 'one rule for one' and that what he did was ok, but now he was an adult, antics such as David and Co. were no longer allowed. As a result, my Dad got a reputation for being grumpy and a bit mad. Not far off the truth in my view!

Back in English, and Mr Gale decided we should expand our English and make a short film. We spent a whole term on making the film which we made up as we went. Somehow or other I ended up playing the part of a girl who was of dubious reputation and often seen kissing boys in shady spots around the school. Everyone thought I was really kissing one of the boys, but I absolutely wasn't! The very thought. Yuk!

This film became something of a legend and it was played over and over for many years at various events. Many years later after I left school, I was regularly reminded it was still in existence, although I imagine it has now been consigned to a skip during some clear out. We all had a lovely time making it and couldn't believe we managed to spin it out for a whole term. The rest of the school watched jealously as we were wandering about outside, while they were all indoors!

One evening, we were all in the car together going somewhere and as Dad reversed off the drive, he reversed back down the road far more than was necessary. In fact, he reversed two house-lengths back. This proved to be deliberate. He had spotted two youths walking up the road and leaning over garden walls breaking off the flower heads of the spring daffodils that were blooming happily. As they approached our next door but one neighbour, he pounced.

Just as they had a handful of flowers in their hands, he shot out of the car, grabbed one of them by the throat, and arm twisted up his back, frogmarched him up to the front door of the house and rang the bell.

Instructing the other one to stay still, which remarkably he did, we were all aghast, not least the poor people whose house it was. They were an elderly couple and opened the door to be faced with my Dad's angry face, holding a young man with one arm up his back and hand around his throat, looking petrified and holding a bunch of daffodils. They were understandably confused!

Dad made the young man tell them what he had done and asked the couple what they wanted to do. I don't think they had the faintest idea other than close the door and hope they would all go away. In the event, Dad asked if they wanted to call the police but they settled for an unreserved apology and promise never to steal or damage their garden again.

Dad reluctantly let him go and got back in the car.

Another time Dad was irked, and surprisingly, I can't remember exactly what had prompted it, but he was in the garage as another two young men committed some misdemeanour. It may have been for dropping litter. He happened to have a hammer in his hand. Dashing out, he also grabbed a crow bar and chased them down the road and around the corner, but they were running faster than he was so as they started to get away, he flung his crow bar and hammer at them catching one of them on the shoulder. Undeterred that he had now assaulted one of them he phoned the police who came and arrested them outside the local shops. It's amazing how attitudes have changed!

Occasionally his behaviour got him into trouble and at some time, someone reported him to the police as being the elusive 'Black Panther' murderer and the police came to interview him. Although we thought he better resembled the Pink Panther, it did rather show he had upset someone greatly. He never found out who it was, and the police somehow knew instantly it wasn't Dad. He may have had many faults but he didn't deserve that accusation.

Biology

Biology was a subject I only did for the first 3 years. I had heard it was hard at 'O' level so decided not to pursue it. However, during our first 3 years, we did learn some things which I have always remembered.

We didn't really know anything about recreational drug use, but during one lesson we were given instructions on how bad they were and told what they did to people who were silly enough to take them. Of all these, I remember vividly being told that anyone who ever took heroine or opium was immediately and forever addicted to the substance, and that their life was then forever ruined as they needed to take ever increasing doses to feel normal. Whilst I have thankfully never been tempted to take drugs, it was powerful advice.

We looked into microscopes and saw the shape of cells in onions and how regular and hexagonal they are. We studied locusts and their ability to wipe out crops in a few hours, along with some real ones that were kept locked in a tank at in the biology lab, which were there to look at and see their breeding cycle. Horrible!

Controversially, I imagine now, we were also given chicken eggs that were fertilised and we had to gently peel some of the shell away, then peel away the inner membrane of variously days-old chicks to study how they developed and see what they looked like which was very unpleasant.

Doing my homework one day, I clearly got in a tangle with mixing evolution with posture. We were shown the archetypal image of an ape and several images following showing how things changed from ape to man and eventually how we were walking upright and on two legs, having also adapted hair and facial features. I mixed that with another lesson about evolution and the size of brain-cavities on various species as we were asked to write an essay on explaining evolution.

Mine proudly concluded, 'Man is cleverer than apes because they have bigger brain cavities and can walk upright.'

When it was returned to me from marking, the comment from the teacher in lovely red ink said, 'Do you normally judge a person's brain power from their ability to stand upright!'

It took a while to work out what the teacher meant, but when the penny finally dropped, I found it really funny.

Music

We studied music for three years. I learned nothing, like most of my classmates. Our teacher I'll call Mr Barker, was a waif-like creature with wispy hair that used to billow as he bounced around the room. He was quite good at playing music and played the rather splendid organ that was in the school hall. When surrounded by children that were interested in music, he came into his own. Unfortunately, when in charge of a big class of not very interested or talented pupils, he was a dreadful. Uninspiring, he had no idea of how to teach and absolutely no ability of how to control a class.

Lessons were boring, he would play a song on the piano, we would then write the words to the song in our text books and that was the lesson. I don't remember ever doing a music exam.

Unfortunately, he had two methods of class control. Shouting, which didn't work, partly because he had such a weak voice and even less authority. The other was equally ineffective but much more painful as he took to hitting people on the back of the head with the wooden handle of his blackboard rubber. This was normally, but not exclusively, meted out to the boys and contrary to his voice, he wasn't weak in delivering the blow.

One day, it all came to a head, literally. He picked on the wrong person and the young man in question stood up, walked out of the classroom without a word and walked out of school. He returned sometime later with his father and from then on, no-one in our class was subjected to the board rubber!

A Field Trip To Edgmond Hall

One of the great things about geography was the field trips. We had two residential trips. One was to Edgmond Hall near Shrewsbury in our early years, and the other was Plas Gwynant in Wales as we started out 'O' levels. On both occasions, I had an incident to remember.

The first one we were in our early years at senior school and we went away for 5 days. Arriving excitedly, I think the place was originally a big house that years later became used for school education trips.

In our eyes, it was located in the middle of nowhere, the night sky was stunning and on a clear night we could see masses of stars in the sky.

The boys and girls had separate dormitories with beds running along either side of the long room. We girls were really pleased to all be sleeping together.

The washing facilities were less appealing as we had to walk outside to an old barn building which still had the circular, old marble, animal watering fountains in it. This was where we all washed together which was a bit of an experience. Having a wash under fine fountain water jets wasn't very easy, but the showers were even less appealing. However, we all managed and survived and we had a wonderful week.

We were, as usual, encouraged to eat all the food on our plates and in between meals we went out and about studying the local flora and fauna. We visited a farm and experienced the aroma of a real working farm as the cow slurry wafted under our noses.

On the last day we were given lunch and as ever there was a big jug of water on each table. Someone had a bright idea that we should have a water drinking competition. The table who could drink the most jugs of water would win. We all filled our glasses and downed the water and refilled them. Our jugs were refilled and so we continued. For some peculiar reason, a rare competitive streak in me woke-up and I wanted our table to win. We were doing very well, but were a bit short. I single-handedly took up the challenge and kept drinking until eventually we were declared winner. The teachers were elsewhere and had no idea of our competition.

Soon after lunch, the coach arrived and with our bags packed we all piled onto the coach and started for home. After a little while, the gentle rocking of the coach, along with the water I had drunk made me think I could do with going to the toilet. I tried shifting about in my seat and loosening my waistband on my trousers and then tried not thinking about it but none of it worked. I wanted a toilet. My friends started to realise my discomfort and within another short space of time, it was becoming urgent. The teachers were told I needed a toilet and after they were assured I couldn't wait until we got back, they asked the coach driver.

For some reason, he was really unhappy to have to stop his coach, let alone have to go out of his way to find a toilet. After much cajoling and prodding, he eventually pulled up at a shabby looking petrol station and as the whole coach giggled and watched, two of my friends had to virtually carry me to the equally shabby toilet. It's one of the few times I wasn't at all bothered what the toilet looked like, I just needed to relieve my poor tortured bladder from an enormous amount of water. Back on the coach, I got a round of applause and lots of mickey taking.

Geography And John Parkes

John Parkes was my geography teacher for 3 years and always around as I went on to study geography at 'O' level, and then at 'A' level. I loved geography. Of all the academic-type subjects, geography was my favourite. Maybe because it was something tangible, the land mass formations, weather, maps, they were all things I could relate to. All the travelling with Mum and Dad made geography come to life.

John also had a great sense of humour. He still does, and it's a testament to his teaching skills and balanced approach to discipline that means we transcended from school and like lots of other people, we have become friends having discovered Facebook.

John loved sweets, and had a nose like a spaniel for them, if he knew we had any, rather than confiscate them, he would allow us to keep them as long as he could have one. I had quite a sweet tooth and he would regularly sniff out my cola cubes, or whatever else I might have secreted away. Cola cubes seemed bigger in those days and very hard, so eating them between lessons was difficult. He would allow us to eat just one too, so it was a win-win treat!

One thing I wasn't keen on was world geography, prairie farming in Saskatchewan didn't do much to pique my interest, although I do remember thinking it must be difficult with all the snow they had in Canada. We also learned that they mined coal there.

In order to aid us, the department has rubber rollers called 'Mercator World Maps.' Printing was prohibitively expensive, so with the aid of an ink pad and roller, we presented our exercise books and John would roll the map onto it. Except, he wasn't very good at it! The page in our exercise book would regularly crumple and crease as he tried to roll it across the page. But amazingly he was very good at getting ink and roller on our hands! As time passed, we realised maybe he wasn't actually bad at it, it was a deliberate act of playing us up!

The geography department was staffed by young teachers who were good fun, the head of the department being a slight exception. His sense of humour was less obvious, especially about himself.

Moving into a different classroom with the head of department as our new teacher, we started 'O' levels. During one lesson, I was sitting with my friend. Our desk looked out onto the square landing area from which each classroom was situated. In the middle, on one side was a toilet, and on the other side a staff room office.

Ours was the only desk in our classroom, from which the classroom opposite could be seen, along with the door to the office.

The phone rang in the office and the teacher in the opposite classroom rushed out to answer it. As he ran out of his room, he went to turn into the office and slipped, next thing he went flying across the landing and landed outside our classroom door. As he got up his head appeared over the glass of our classroom door, he looked a bit dazed and confused as to why he was on the floor instead of answering the phone in the office. He looked around to see if anyone had seen him.

Unluckily for him, we had... and it was incredibly funny...and I started to laugh...and I couldn't stop!

Although it was a bit of a 'had to be there moment,' even now when I think about it, I can still laugh uncontrollably, but being in the classroom with Mr Fisher who hadn't got a sense of humour wasn't going to end well. The more I tried to stop laughing, the worse it became and eventually the whole class was in fits of laughter, but they had no idea what they were laughing at, which just made me worse. Eventually, the class was in chaos. Mr Fisher had been pushed over the edge, lost his temper and threatened us all with detention if we didn't be quiet.

Plas Gwynant

The next incident was at Plas Gwynant, in Wales. Just after the start of the school year in September 1977, we went on a field trip. It was to be the highlight of our first year of 'O' level geography. We were really excited and were accompanied by some of the geography department staff. We were really looking forward to it.

Once we arrived, we were shown to our dormitories and this time there were four beds to a room. Bunk beds this time and the ground floor rooms were for us girls and the boys were directly above us on the first floor. We settled into our groups and unpacked.

We were given a short guided-tour and then after all the rules of what we could and couldn't do, we went off to eat. It was a room with a canteen style buffet and we queued in line to fill our plates. There was a rule. Eat what you want but once it's on your plate, you have to eat it all.

This was a very easy rule. It made sure people didn't pile their plates high with food and then waste it, but the only flaw was that if you had something on it that you didn't like it was too late. And of course, there were several experiences of that. Mainly the boys I hasten to add. One particular night one of the boys had a plate of food and there were things on it he didn't want to eat. It was absolutely forbidden to hand back a plate with food on it, so he ended up with all the extra food in his pockets. Mushed sprouts and potato oozing with dripping gravy, seeped from his pockets as he left the dining room and ran back to discharge it all down the nearest toilet.

One night as we came out from eating, I was walking with my friends and we were stopped by the head of department. The man with a limited sense of humour. Mr Fisher. He said he wanted a word and for a few moments we were all confused and especially when it turned out he wanted to speak to me. He said I owed him an apology. I hadn't got a clue what for, or what I'd done.

'On the way into eat, I made a remark and do you remember what you said to me?'

I was confused.

'Do you know what you called me?' he growled.

'Er, No, Sir.' I replied.

'You called me a rat!' he steamed, and then stood back arms folded with a glint of satisfaction on his face as though he had caught me out.

'Oh, right.' I replied a bit nonplussed.

'Well, what do you say to that?' He asked, hands now on his hips and leaning forward slightly.

'I don't know Sir.' I replied

'Well, do you call your mother and father a rat?' he asked.

'Yes, Sir.' I replied. At this point I thought he was in danger of combusting, but I still didn't understand what I had said that was wrong. Clearly nonplussed he paused before saying,

'Well, don't call me a rat again.'

'Ok, Sir.' I said.

We all walked away absolutely confused and Mr Fisher looked very uncomfortable. In those days, calling people a rat was just one of those sayings we all used. It didn't mean anything bad or offensive. It just was something we said in response to all manner of things. Mr Fisher clearly didn't know about this and was seriously offended. I had to make a special effort not to call him a rat again.

The next day, we went for a walk, part way up Snowdon. We were given rucksacks which had a packed lunch, cagoules and all other necessary equipment, and off we went. The weather was lovely and the scenery was stunning and slowly but surely, we made our way up and up. After a while, my friend and I both started to feel tired. Our rucksacks felt heavy on our backs but no one else seemed to be complaining or tired so we plodded on. Eventually we stopped for something to eat and unpacked our lunch. Imagine our delight as we discovered we both had a rather large boulder wrapped neatly at the bottom of our rucksacks. A little joke from the teachers!

Although he wasn't there in person, John Parkes had managed to join us in spirit having had a hand in the idea!

The next day, we walked into Beddgelert and back. On the way back, it was quite muddy and as we plodded our way around the puddles, some were unavoidable. We tried dodging around one particularly boggy area taking it in turns and then it was me. I slipped and ended up knee deep in mud. You can imagine the ribbing I got from everyone, including the staff!

A few months after we came back from Plas Gwynant, one day we got to lessons and were told we were doing something different. Our geography classes went onto the square landing outside the rooms and a cassette player emerged. Two of our classmates were learning to dance, and so they were invited to demonstrate what they had learned by dancing around the landing. They were very good and travelled all over the country competing. It was lovely.

At the end, I was then invited to the centre of the circle and given an envelope. It was my birthday. I had no idea they knew and inside there was a card. I was invited to read it out loud.

On the front of it were cartoon drawings of different noses, with the words, 'When you have finished picking your nose, have a piece of birthday cake!'

Inside were several poems that the staff had written.

'Jack and Gill went up the hill to study glaciation, their journey down was a slow foxtrot, they danced in rock formation!'

Another read. 'There was a young lady called Gill, who went for a walk up a hill, she fell in a boggy it made her feel soggy and never went there again!'

One day, I was in my maths class. Our teacher was quite young and not very experienced. He wasn't brilliant at class control and was very old fashioned in his style of dress. A bit of a geek really. Looking out of the window, John Parkes and another geography teacher were walking towards the school block and saw me.

They started making small gestures to me when my maths teacher wasn't looking. One finger either side of their nose, it was a subliminal two fingers gesture. They did it several times and were giggling. I couldn't help it, I did it back and they did the same. In the end, I just gave them both a 'V' sign and next thing they were at the door to the classroom.

Opening the door they said, 'Mr Southwood, Gillian Skidmore has just made a rude hand sign to us.'

Mr Southwood was furious! 'Skidmore, get out!' he yelled.

'But Sir, they started it!'

'I don't want to hear it, get out!'

I obediently got up and left the room. The two teachers were giggling on the stairs and after telling me they hoped I didn't get into too much trouble, they went!

After a few minutes, Mr Southwood came out and gave me a severe telling off.

'I do not expect a young lady such as yourself to be seen making rude gestures out of my window. In fact, I don't expect you to be doing that anywhere!' He admonished.

'Yes, Sir. Sorry Sir, but they started it! They made rude gestures to me first.'

'Don't be ridiculous, just get back in the classroom and get on with your work.' He said.

I walked back into the room and was met by a huge round of applause from my classmates. Immediately, Mr Southwood saw red and threw me out again!

After another few minutes he came out and told me off again. Despite my protestations that I couldn't be responsible for my classmates' applause, he said if I hadn't played up, they wouldn't have done it, so as a punishment I had to do a detention!

It's the one and only time I ever did a detention. I didn't dare tell Mum, and especially not Dad. I made my friends come and wait around for me as he made me clean the windows and ponder my behaviour. I'm not sure who was more uncomfortable, me cleaning windows being watched, or him not quite knowing what to do with himself as I cleaned. Once I'd done enough, he let me out with a stern warning of 'don't let it happen again!'

The geography teachers were very amused but even so, they weren't prepared to admit their part in it all!

Along with our good-humoured fun, I think on the whole, we were a good year group. All of our teachers, not just geography, liked us and this was born out years later as we grew up and met up with some of them in our adult life. They confirmed we were a good year group, and nowadays thanks to the wonder of social media we are in touch again.

John Parkes still has a wicked sense of humour, an amazing memory for all the pranks and fun we all had, and especially enjoys winding me up at any opportunity! I feel so lucky that we had such a sense of fun and laughter, whilst knowing always where the boundaries lay. It worked both ways.

Back to Reality & A Diet For Life

After a lovely 5 day trip to Plas Gwynant, we packed up our things and came back home happy and refreshed. I remember so much about that trip, probably because it was to be the last of my childhood carefree times.

Back home and on a lovely high, the next day was a Saturday. Dad seemed agitated, but he wasn't in a bad mood, just a bit odd. He persuaded me to go with him to see my Nan. I didn't really want to go as I really wanted to see my friend to chat over and replay the events of Plas Gwynant, but at his insistence, in the end I went. Arriving at Nan's, she seemed agitated too and I felt a bit uncomfortable.

Once we were all in the lounge, Dad said,

'Your Mum has cancer, she doesn't know, and she only has 3 months to live.' Then he just seemed to stare at me, and so did Nan.

I wasn't sure what I was supposed to do or say. I felt very uncomfortable at the amount of attention they were giving me and I just wanted to get away from them both. The whole scenario felt so orchestrated and false, it really didn't register. It was just very surreal and out of context. All I really wanted to do was go home and go to see my friend, but they just seemed to be staring at me, so in the end I tried to force a few tears as I thought this was probably the reaction they were waiting for. I was made to promise that I wouldn't tell Mum and try to act normally. This was neither easy nor hard since I felt nothing, other than odd.

In those days, it was quite the norm for people to be kept in the dark about their impending fate, the decision being left for the family to decide as to whether the soon-to-be-deceased person was to be educated into their own demise. Thankfully, it didn't last long and Mum knew in her own mind long before she was told formally what was happening, but it all became much easier when we all knew the truth and could be open about it.

For some reason, I'm not sure why, I only told two of my friends just then, and later I told another one or two. All the way through the rest of school, I didn't really tell anyone about Mum being on borrowed time.

It all came about when Mum and Dad decided to go on a diet. Dad went to get under the sink to turn off the water so he could change a washer on the tap and found he couldn't fit in very well, so it was time to do something. They both had a few pounds to lose and so they began to diet together.

They started the egg and grapefruit 'Commando' diet, which guarantees weight loss, if you have the stomach for it. Raw eggs aren't the most appetising thing to start the day with, but Mum did it religiously, along with lots of dry toast, protein, cottage cheese, and grapefruit. Dad wasn't quite as strict about it and of course he stuck to having his cheese sandwich at night and didn't have the raw eggs. (I don't blame him!) Dad generally cut out all the rubbish and he lost weight. Mum didn't lose anything. In fact, she put some more on.

She was also having 'women's problems' as they called it in those days. I remember being with her one day as she was talking to a neighbour and hearing them talking in half sentences so that I didn't understand what was being said. I got the gist though that something wasn't right and the neighbour told Mum she must go to see the doctor which she did. I later found out she was having very heavy periods and eventually went to the doctor. In no time at all she was in hospital having a hysterectomy and 'had it all taken away.' Unfortunately, they also found she had cancer.

We went to visit her after her operation at Hallam Hospital. It was an old Victorian ward and as we walked in, Mum was in a bed on the left. She looked well, but tired. She stayed in for a week and then came home. Mum and Dad must have gone back after a time to get the results and this was when Dad was told. Mum had cancer, it had spread and she was going to die.

It's hard to imagine these days that the patient wouldn't be told this, but in those days, the relative was given the news and had the decision as to whether to tell the patient. For the time being Dad chose not to tell Mum that she was going to die. I imagine the shock was so much to come to terms with for himself, he wasn't able to do anything.

There then followed a series of trips to the Queen Elizabeth hospital for radiotherapy in the hope that it would help extend her time left and a course of chemotherapy. She was very unhappy at being tattooed for the radiotherapy equipment. Following this, she was admitted to the Queen Elizabeth hospital and the chemotherapy was administered there as an in-patient. I didn't like visiting her there as the whole experience felt uncomfortable. The hospital felt strange and sitting around her bed, trying to chat to fill in time was awkward. I was happy when she came home. The chemotherapy left her tired and ironically, she lost lots of weight but looked awful.

Mum never complained throughout her illness, but once or twice, something happened that would really affect her. After a couple of doses of chemotherapy, the inevitable happened as Mum woke up one morning to find her hair all over the pillow. She was devastated as you would expect. It was a weekday and we were all out, Mum was home alone. I came home from school and Mum was in tears. Sobbing uncontrollably, it is one of the saddest times I ever felt for her. She had woken up in the morning and as she lifted her head off the pillow, the pillowcase was covered in her hair. As she went to brush it, it fell out and filled her brush. Mum was distraught and felt broken-hearted. During all the things she so bravely endured, this was her worst time. Unable to stop crying, she had spent the day in a bit of a blur and somehow knocked the ill-fated TV off its stand as she tried to switch it on. The sight of Mum sobbing as the TV lay face down, looking equally distraught is an image I will always remember. She cried some more until Dad came home, picked it up and switched it back on again. Fortunately, it still worked.

She had a wig made which was beautiful. Nothing like her own hair, she had one made that she liked the style of and it was made of real hair to boot! The downside was that it made her head itch and she would regularly shove a knitting needle into it to scratch her head as she was knitting. Unfortunately, it suffered a mishap as she opened the oven door and it melted the front. She had it repaired but always took it off when she was cooking and wore a pair of old tights on her head instead. I've no idea where this idea came from but it didn't seem unusual at the time.

After the chemo and several check-ups at the QE, we had some good news. Mum was in remission and given the all clear. The death sentence was lifted for a while. Her bright and colourful-self reappeared and she went on a bit of a shopping spree buying some new clothes. Mum loved colour and it's something I've definitely inherited.

When we were going out anywhere, she would squeeze herself into a longline bra, which covered her to the waist, then wriggle into a ridiculously tight panty-girdle and once her dress was on, she looked lovely with a shapely curvy figure. On the way back, she would undo her bra, and releasing herself from her vice-like panty-girdle as soon as she could, she would expand back to her normal-sized self.

Mum and Dad took these opportunities to go out and about on holiday, days out, visiting people as much as they could, and made the very best of the time they had together, without us girls.

Mum was quite deaf in one ear and if she went to bed during the day and was lying on her one side, she would never hear the doorbell so Chris and I were given a house key. Chris lost more keys than you could imagine, so was always having spares cut although we never told Dad and if they were out, we used to hide a key in case we got locked out.

With Mum and Dad out and about so often, Chris and I were careful never to let many people know when they went away, as we were worried a throng of people would arrive for a party that we hadn't arranged, and the house would end up in tatters. It happened quite often in those days. Even when parents agreed to a house party, things often ended up broken or damaged. The most common damage was when the boys arrived with a can of 'Party 6,' a big can of beer that would have inevitably been shaken about as it was transported to the party. As they pierced it with a can opener, the contents would explode all over the ceiling before they could get another hole in it to equalise the pressure. A lesson in both physics and chemistry, it was best dealt with by placing a tea towel over it until all the fizz subsided.

After a while, life fell into a different sort of normality. Mum was ill, but we all got on with it and carried on living. It was a good way to be. We didn't wander around being miserable or make any dramatic changes to our daily life. I have no idea whether they told the teachers at school, but I don't think they did and school seemed unchanged. I asked John Parkes later if he knew and he didn't, so I suspect not.

The Walking Club

As we got older, we became part of a walking club. Organised by one of the teachers, and ably abetted by two others, we formed a group. Also included in the group to begin with, was my Godmother's daughter so although Dad wasn't really keen, reason unknown, he couldn't really refuse.

We were really lucky that in those days, common sense prevailed. Health and Safety didn't exist and we were encouraged to take responsibility for ourselves and those around us. The group ebbed and flowed a bit and evolved with more people joining us and a few people moving on.

I learned to orienteer quite well. Map-reading on the ground, so to speak, noting the distance between contour lines to see how steep land mass was rising and giving an outline of the topography, I also learned to use a compass. We had some marvellous times and I still like looking at maps.

Recently, I persuaded my husband to go to London to a map exhibition after seeing it on the morning news. He wasn't as keen as me, but we were both impressed by the wide variety of maps, originals such as the one written by A.A Milne, showing Pooh Corner, the first one of the dark side of the moon, and a very lovely topographic map of the oceans. Not everyone's idea of fun, I grant you, but we enjoyed the day. When they say 'every day is a learning day,' I learned that the tube map showing straight lines and regular corners, isn't how it actually looks in real life. Being used to knowing a road map shows the actual shape of the road, and train lines on maps following an accurate route, I assumed the tube map would be the same. It was a revelation to me to find that it wasn't!

Twice, at February half term, we went to Trawsfynnedd in Wales. It was a cottage. No running water, no electricity, in fact, it was really just a stone cottage with rooms, and a kitchen. It had Calor-gas for the cooker and lights, an open fire, a hand pump to draw water up and that was about it.

It was another wonderful place to see the stars at night. No light pollution, the cottage was 3 miles off the nearest road and was completely isolated. Several times we sat outside in the evenings as the various stars and constellations were pointed out to us. I loved looking at them even though I could never remember many of them!

The more we stared up, the more stars emerged.

My friend Jackie and I were always being 'picked' on by our teachers to play us up. It was called having fun. Nothing terrible, no bullying, and whilst it may seem outrageous now, we just had light hearted fun. I can't remember what started it, but it became a game of get them back for whatever was last done to us. Jackie was very clever academically, but sometimes inadvertently used to set herself up a bit, and on one trip to the Lake District, brought her baby-doll nightie along. The lads got hold of it somehow and the next thing it was flying from the top of the aerial on the minibus for everyone in the Youth Hostel to admire.

During one February half term, it was time for us to exact revenge. Invariably, I used to think up the ideas, and Jackie used to try to execute them.

The first thing I did this time was to buy some Ex-Lax chocolate. If you don't know what it is, it is a laxative, carefully wrapped up in chocolate.

We got to the cottage on the first night and Jackie and I made a massive effort to make sure we were allowed to do the cooking. (No flans though!) We were both very able to cook and we made a stew and followed it up with apple pie and custard. As we served the custard, we carefully melted the whole of the little bar of chocolate into one bowl and served it to the one teacher who created most of the mischief. It was only a small bar, but contained some special ingredient... Senna.

And then we waited...

And waited...

And then decided it hadn't worked so put it down to experience.

Next day, as became the norm, one of the teachers would stay behind to drive the minibus to meet us at a forward point of where we walked. This particular day, it was over the Roman Steps and along the way until we eventually ended up at Betws-y-Coed. That evening we were going to go through the tunnels for a bit of light hearted fun.

The tunnels were remnants from the old railway and you could walk along them. At some point midway, it became pitch black as the bend in the tunnel blocked out light from either end. It was so much fun being spooked by people falling about and bouncing off walls.

When we got back from the tunnels, we were met by the teacher who had stayed behind, and coincidentally, was the one we had served the chocolate custard to.

He looked awful. Grey, holding his abdomen and groaning about being in pain, he was in quite a lot of distress. The doors of the minibus were open, to let the odour of his abdominal gas escape!

He was suffering from chronic diarrhoea, and had no idea why, although he seemed to think we may have poisoned him with our food the previous night. We denied it emphatically and pointed out everyone else was fine, and it had all been served from the same big pot so it couldn't have been from us. Amazingly he believed us, but he was so affected, he couldn't walk with us for two days as he couldn't leave the safety of the bathroom far behind!

We realised the tiny bar of chocolate packed a powerful punch!

Whilst we were in Betws-y-Coed, we went to a local pub, and there we played spoon duelling. This involved two people sitting opposite one another with a spoon in their mouth. In turn they would lower their head and the opponent would use as much force as they could muster and hit the other person on the head with their spoon. But like any good pub game, there was a twist to it, as everyone, except the one spoon dueller, knew the rules. So, as the blissfully unaware spoon dueller lowered their head, the referee would gently hit them on the top of the head with a small bottle! Not overly hard, just enough to make them wince. Believing this was caused by the spoon from the opponent, they would take their turn, mustering every ounce of strength before delivering a blow to the head. The opponent would squeal and complain about the pain they were experiencing and then swap turns again. Of course, you cannot obtain any amount of force from holding a spoon in your mouth, so the only person who really got any sort of pain, was the person who didn't know the game. After a suitable amount of time, the game would end and occasionally, they would be let in on the joke.

One morning, Jackie and I were asked if we would go and get some milk. We agreed, it was a lovely day and it meant we could have a nice walk while everyone else did chores in the cottage. Off we went to meet the milkman that we were told would be arriving at the farm about 2 miles along the lane back towards the main road. Half way there we stated to feel something was amiss, but weren't quite sure what, but we wandered along chatting and enjoying the walk. We arrived at the end of the drive to the farm and a mad sheepdog came galloping towards us barking like a banshee and baring its teeth. Following behind came the farmer who asked us what we wanted.

We told him we were here to meet the milkman, but he hadn't arrived yet. He told us there wasn't one. We were confused and then farmer said, I'm a farmer, we don't need a milkman!

Ding! The light came on and we realised we had been set up. The farmer found it really amusing and we had no option but to walk back and face the humiliation that they had got us good and proper. However, not wanting to waste an opportunity, we came up with some more plans of how to get them back. We didn't need to wait long.

Foolishly, one of the teachers decided to go down to the stream that ran outside the cottage and have a wash al fresco. I got my camera and sent Jackie down towards the water. The teacher was a bit twitchy as to what she was up to, but we reassured him, we were just taking a photo. Naively, he bent down to have a wash and quick as a flash, Jackie pushed him in! I got a great picture of it, (which has since disappeared) and he was absolutely furious, wet through, and cold. Considering he liked to play tricks on us, on this occasion he had a surprising lack of humour when it was the other way around!

Twice whilst we were at the cottage, we were allowed to visit Trawsfynnedd nuclear power station. We walked to it across the hills and were taken on a guided tour.

By the end of the visit, we were all convinced nuclear energy was safe and the way forward.

I remember them telling us, they raised the nuclear rods in the reactors to reduce energy production and lowered them to increase it, and in the unlikely event that things went wrong, they would sprinkle boron dust all over the reactor and the whole thing would be shut down safely.

We were then shown the turbines and then the lovely lake that had the residual water recycled back into it to cool. Since it had a slightly higher temperature, the lake was home to a thriving population of trout.

We were also lucky enough to visit a Hydro-Electric power station once too. I really enjoyed that, and the principle of how it worked so simply was something I really thought clever. Even better that at the end of the day, they used their own electricity to pump the water back up to the top lake ready for the next day's electricity generation.

We went all over the country on our trips, we climbed Snowdon, Cader Idris, Scafell and Scafell Pike, Helvellyn, we walked the Ridgeway, part of the South Downs, various parts of the Pennine way and Brecon Beacons as well as various Welsh mountains.

Climbing Snowdon was a wonderful experience and we were rewarded by a wonderful view as the clouds cleared long enough for us to see for miles across the glorious landscape. Coming down was much quicker as we came careering down the scree slopes and learned the art of scree-jumping. Something that would probably be banned as too risky these days.

We also went to Bigbury-On-Sea. We had a fabulous weekend there staying in a youth hostel and although we didn't do much walking, we had a wonderful few days away. I never forgot Bigbury and it is still a favourite place to visit with my husband. We love to have something to eat and a coffee from The Pilchard pub in front of the Burgh Island Hotel and even though these days it's always outrageously expensive, it's a wonderful spot to just sit and watch the world go by.

I regularly feel so lucky to have been at school during the times we were there. Nowadays, some of the things we did wouldn't even get into the thought process, let alone do. One of which was a night hike!

I'm not exactly sure where we went, but I think it may have been near Much Wenlock, because the idea was that at the end of the hike we would go to a place called Hill Top and watch the sun rise. It definitely wasn't Hill Top, West Bromwich!

We all met at school, piled excitedly into the mini bus, and off we went. We started off at a pub somewhere, had a drink, (not alcohol) and something to eat and then as it closed, we set off.

It was a clear night and perfect for seeing the stars and watching the night sky, as the beautiful moonlight lit our way. We walked for several hours, sipped on a little tot or two of homemade parsnip wine which someone had brought in a hip flask, and were chased by a herd of curious cows as we crossed through their field.

We were told to ignore them, they wouldn't chase us, and were just curious creatures. We tried to ignore them and just keep walking. We were told not to run, because then they would start too, but it was very difficult to ignore our instinct as they approached us. Being so big and powerful, we didn't trust that they just wanted to come and say hello! As they walked more quickly, so did we. The gate at the other end of the field was quite a distance away so although we walked steadily in a line, we started to speed up a bit. The cows joined in and eventually, we all started to run as the cows gave chase! Although they had pretty much surrounded us, we just got to the gate before them.

I still have no idea if they were just being curious or if they would have run into us, but I can only say it felt better to be safe than sorry, and even if they had just been curious, the drool and slobber that they produced wouldn't have been welcome all over us!

At the end of the night, we were all completely exhausted. We hadn't slept for nearly 24 hours. Undeterred though, as we got to the mini-bus the teacher who was driving was still keen for us to see the sunrise at Hill Top!

Everyone got in and most fell asleep in a few minutes, but someone needed to navigate the map to Hill Top so I volunteered. Having learned orienteering skills over time, I was pleased with the opportunity to test my map reading skills, as roads were much easier than land and footpaths.

It was one of the most difficult things I had ever done. Being beyond the pale of tiredness, trying to think, read and navigate was so hard. With the rest of the minibus asleep, we found our way. I can still hear the words, 'We need to get to Hill Top to see the sun come up!'

Driving through an avenue of trees, eventually we emerged at Hill Top! We woke everyone up and after several grunts and groans, we all watched the sun rise. Slightly unimpressed due to the overwhelming tiredness we all felt, after a few minutes, everyone was back asleep. I was in the front of the mini-bus with my friend and did my best to stay awake as we headed home. I was worried the driver might drop off too. By the time we were dropped off it was early morning. I crawled into my lovely comfortable bed and slept for most of the day.

I can't say I would want to do a night hike again, but it was a wonderful experience. We stopped regularly to listen to the silence of nothingness, except for the night creatures we could hear rustling around. The change to the landscape colours we saw from the light of the stars and the moon were wonderful being so different to the daytime. It was a memory to treasure.

April Fool

One year, April fool loomed and I was talking to Jackie about what we could do.

We decided to play a trick on Mr Henson. Our Chemistry teacher at the time, he looked and acted very old for his age, and had a very shiny bald head. He also didn't have the best sense of humour. Fodder for our trick!

The idea was so flimsy, but simple. Jackie would knock her pen over the teacher's large bench-desk in the chemistry lab, and then ask Mr Henson to pass her pen back.

As he bent down to retrieve it, I would rip a piece of fabric and then tell him he had split his trousers. What could go wrong?

As it happens, nothing went wrong, in fact it all went superbly right and as we screamed, 'Sir, you've ripped your trousers,' Mr Henson ran out of the classroom to go and check himself.

Realising too late it was a trick, let alone realising he had his long lab coat on so we wouldn't have seen anyway, he came back in looking extremely red-faced and embarrassed at having fallen for our little trick.

In geography, a few weeks later, Jackie and I somehow managed to find a way of getting out of wandering about outside at lunchtime, by volunteering to do some work to help the department. This time, we didn't need the fabric, as we managed to get one of the younger teachers to bend down and his trousers really did split all along the seam from front to back. This particular day though the sun was shining and he had to walk all across the school to needlework to get his trousers repaired wearing a huge Sou'wester to cover his modesty.

We weren't naughty, we were just a bit mischievous. Nothing terrible, and no malice, but we had a good sense of fun and fairness and knew where the boundaries were. It all worked both ways.

I often reflect, how these days, between us we would be either sacked, expelled, imprisoned or counselled, in what we saw and experienced as our gentle, happy, innocent fun! It was all educational, rubbed any sharp edges off us and was character forming. Some wonderful moments in time.

One very embarrassing incident I was inadvertently instigator of was in Chemistry.

Lots of us went to see West Bromwich Albion play at home, sometimes Saturdays and sometimes a weekday evening kick-off. The atmosphere was great and whilst Dad was very anti me going, Mum was more enthusiastic having been a season ticket holder in her younger days.

We loved going and enjoyed the feeling of all the people walking en masse back to West Bromwich town centre afterwards. Consequently, we all wanted a WBA football scarf. They weren't cheap and Mum offered to knit me one, but I wanted a 'real' one and so eventually she bought me one from Siviter Sports shop.

I loved it! it was very soft to wear and the white stripes against the blue looked the real deal. We all wore them in a particular way which was the height of fashion.

During physics lessons, as in chemistry, for health and safety reasons, (yes, we did have some H&S rules,) we all used to put our coats and scarves at the back of the room on a long bench. After the lesson I went to collect mine and my scarf was missing. A good hunt around and there was no sign of it. No-one admitted to seeing it as we then went to chemistry.

Mr Moody was the Chemistry teacher and somehow got to know my scarf was missing. He asked everyone to check if they had picked up my scarf by mistake but no one had. It was looking like someone had stolen it and I had a good idea who it was, but no-one was prepared to admit it.

He said he wasn't going to teach us until someone found my scarf, but as no one did, we sat in silence all lesson. I was embarrassed, but most people found it quite nice to sit and do nothing for 40 minutes. We were dismissed and told someone had better find my scarf and return it to me.

Going home and telling Mum my scarf was missing added to my misery as she hit the roof!

She threatened all sorts, didn't seem at all to see it wasn't my fault since we had been told to leave our things at the back of the physics room and said if it didn't turn up, she was going to go down to the school and complain to the headmaster. I thought this was the most awful thing as I didn't want to raise a big fuss, but she was having none of it. She eventually agreed she wouldn't go down if I reported it to the office and made it known. I wished I had just said I lost it, but next day I duly went to the office and asked if someone had handed it in and reported it missing. No such luck! They had lots of scarves but none were mine.

Back in chemistry Mr Moody was also unimpressed it was still missing and we spent another lesson in silence. He told us we would not be taught any lessons until my scarf turned up, so for two weeks we sat during eight lessons in silence. I was mortified with embarrassment.

Eventually, my friends and I had a plan. We went to the office and asked if they had any WBA scarves which were unclaimed and they found one. We all pretended it was mine and Mum and Mr Moody were happy and life returned to normal. I knew it wasn't my scarf but I was so pleased the ordeal was over! Maybe it was penance for the April Fool trick!

As I have mentioned, I loved sport at school, I still do, which is lucky for my husband who also loves sport. At junior school I learned to climb a rope, which always looked easy until you had to do it. It took lots of practice knotting it around your feet and learning the technique of hauling yourself up, but I persevered and felt very pleased to have got to the top.

I also enjoyed gymnastics. We were lucky to have after school clubs that we could attend and I proudly got several gymnastics badges for achieving various poses and somersaults, the BAGA awards, British Amateur Gymnastics Awards. My favourite was trampolining although I wasn't good enough to be picked for the team. We can't all be good at everything and I believe that taking part involves much more than the end result since without the also-ran's, there wouldn't be a race. We all have different strengths and weaknesses and we should embrace them all equally as it makes us more rounded as a human being. Likewise, competition is good and should be encouraged as a good thing. So many things in life outside of sport are competitive, applying for jobs, promotion, the ability to deal with not winning or being great at something is a very important life lesson, as is just the ability to enjoy something just because you can.

Dad had no interest in sport. He did enjoy swimming and ice-skating, so this was the nearest he came to being sporty. Mum was the opposite and loved all sports.

Every week, the council allowed its workers to have exclusive access to the swimming baths. Dad started to take us swimming. The first time we arrived, we got in the water and paddled about. A little while later and Dad turned his back for a minute and I was off. Straight up to the top board and ready to jump. It's a trait and habit that has followed me through my life, although these days I try to stop and think first. Thankfully, on this particular occasion, I didn't get chance to jump as Dad came rushing after me and stopped me from taking the plunge.

We were also lucky enough to be taken to Bearwood Ice-rink on regular occasions, and Dad glided round very elegantly on his own skates as my sister and I learned to stand up, fall over, try again and eventually get the hang of skating. One Christmas we also got a pair of roller skates each. Flying down the drive into the road was great fun, and sometimes, with a following wind and plenty of gusto, we would end up at the top of our neighbour's drive opposite. It took quite a while to learn how to negotiate turns and stopping, which resulted in a few bumps and scrapes along the way before we became proficient on our little wheels.

Although Dad wasn't very sporty, he was very adventurous, far more than Mum was, and encouraged us to be the same. At one point I was really keen to do a parachute jump and although Dad was all for it, Mum was very against it and because she was quite poorly at the time, I didn't do it.

Learning Household Chores

Whilst Mum was poorly, me at the age of 14, and my sister Christine being two and a half years older, had to learn to run the house. Mum's idea of letting us do as little as possible had to go and although Mum had taught us lots of skills, we now 'had' to do things rather than 'choose' to do them.

To begin with Chris wanted to do the cooking and washing and I was to do the cleaning. Chris wanted to be a cookery teacher so it meant she could practice her skills. Unfortunately, this had a few downsides in that sometimes things didn't go according to plan.

The clues should have been there. One day when we were quite young, Mum had a rare migraine. She had to go to bed to lie down and Chris, being older decided to take charge and make me tea. Boiled egg and soldiers. She knew how to make it and boiled the egg for three minutes precisely and then served it to me. Taking the top off the egg it was still raw. Chris was so indignant that she had done it properly she made me eat it and only later found out she should have brought it up to boil first, before starting the three minutes.

As we got older, Chris went out for a meal and had trout on the bone for the first time. She loved it so much, she went and bought a whole trout to cook. I told her she needed to gut it, as I had seen how Mum had done it when she bought fish, but Chris was adamant her fish had been whole in every sense. After grilling it for a while, she became a bit nervous about it, so we went to one of our neighbours who was a lecturer at the Birmingham college of food and domestic art, complete with grill-pan and fish. She told us we needed to gut it first. We went back and Chris spent some time squeezing and prodding it until eventually, she managed to gut it. Unsurprisingly, she didn't enjoy it anywhere near as much as she expected to!

When Chris did cook though, she was rather good at it, but it wasn't something she did on a daily basis, preferring Heinz toast toppers, which were quick and easy, a favourite being chicken and mushroom. Eventually, we changed roles, Chris did the washing and I did the cooking making Sunday lunch most weeks. I got to be very good at it and used to make enough gravy for Dad to have for several days ahead. If he ran out, he would heat up a tin of Heinz beef soup and put that on his dinner. Even now, I am very pleased to be able to say, I do make rather decent gravy. My husband says no-one can make a meal out of nothing quicker than me and I put that down to all the practice.

Thankfully, for the children who would have been under Chris's charge, she decided against being a home economics teacher. She wouldn't have been a good tutor as she had absolutely no interest in children and very little patience to explain things. I often refer to my sister as akin to the child catcher in Chitty-Chitty Bang-Bang!

She was however very good at art. She went to Ingestre Hall with the school for a week when she was 14 and came back with a huge piece of modern art which had impressed the teachers no end. Dad however looked at it rather differently, well from every angle to be honest, but he didn't really get it. It is representative of the sun, moon, stars, night and day and about 4 feet tall. At home it was hung overlooking the stairs for many years until we all moved out. It was then parcelled up and never saw the light of day until I asked her in recent years if I could have it. She gave it to me and it now hangs in pride of place in my clinic.

Later, after Mum died, she did another painting. It is on a white background with short black lines all over it at different angles, and the bottom right-hand corner is plain white. Dad didn't get that one either, he just thought it was unfinished and never understood what it was about.

Meantime, back doing housework, Saturday and Sunday were household chore days. Cooking, cleaning, shopping, washing, ironing and whatever else there was to do.

Chris and I agreed that we would split things and to begin with that was fine. After a while we changed things around as we found out things we preferred to do and some things we shared, so I'm not saying I did everything, because I didn't, but my experiences of the jobs I did is here. Chris also discovered a love of gardening which dad was very grateful for as he had a bad back and so gardening was something that he found difficult, plus, I think he hated weeding!

During the week, we tended to make our own food. Chris and I would often make and share our tea, and Dad used to have sandwiches for tea. He used to eat his main meal at lunchtime like lots of people in those days so this wasn't something that changed because of Mum, he always had sandwiches for tea. Often lettuce, (yes, just lettuce!) or cheese or ham. Rarely more than one item was between the two rounds of Hovis. Occasionally he would make a mistake and eat cabbage instead as he couldn't always tell the difference between lettuce and cabbage.

When Mum was first poorly, Dad couldn't even make a cup of tea. Mum taught him how and then introduced him to the pressure cooker. He learned how to do everything in the pressure cooker, from stewing apples to making a whole meal in one pot.

We had 3 fruit trees in the garden, apple, pear and plum, so each year we would harvest the fruit and it would be stewed in the pressure cooker and eaten, often just on its own and although the idea of that sounds unpleasant now, it was rather nice at the time. Sometimes we would have ice cream or custard to go with it, Chris always liked Carnation cream, but I didn't like cream and ice cream used to give me the 'ice-cream headache' so I usually had custard.

As Dad became adept with the pressure cooker, occasionally he would have an accident, the valve would explode and we would have stewed fruit all over the ceiling. (I'm glad it was him that did it and not me!)

He would come home for dinner at lunch time, which in those days was called dinner time, and put a pork chop, tinned potatoes and tinned peas into the pressure cooker, cook it for 20 minutes and then put it on a plate. I can't say it was ever very appetising to look at but he seemed to enjoy it. The pork chop looked white and insipid, and the already cooked peas and potatoes were reduced to wrinkled and watery looking mush.

Cleaning on Saturdays was a chore and something that I think had a profound effect on me in later life. I can't say I didn't enjoy it, but it's something that caused some strife as Dad seemed to complain about it! I would start in the dining room, duster in hand and polish in the other, I had a routine of what I did, which when I left home, made cleaning difficult, as I never seemed to be able to follow a 'path' around the house in the same way as previously.

In subsequent houses it meant I never felt the whole house was cleaned all together and even now, it's rare for me to feel like the house is 'properly clean' as I can't do it all in one go. I'm not OCD, (although my husband might disagree!) I think I'm like most women, we like a clean home and unless I can clean every surface in one day, it would never feel completely clean to me.

I don't stress over it, quite the opposite, I enjoy cleaning and if I am feeling stressed I find it relaxing and drift off into a complete world of my own. There is something very rewarding in it, it's tangible and satisfying to me. The trouble is, I can easily spend a couple of hours cleaning something like the cooker hood and Karen, our cleaner can do the whole house and the clinic in three hours! I must point out that I don't spend hours doing housework, but when I do it, I make a big impression on it!

Back home with Mum and Dad, I would start in the dining room. We had a table, sideboard, TV, chairs and an old TV cabinet which was used as a cupboard. The fireplace was a typical 1950's tiled hearth and there were plugs on either side of the fireplace and one behind the TV. One of the plugs next to the fireplace had a surface pattress box which had a streak of gloss paint on it. The paint was so glued to the socket, no matter how I tried, I never managed to get it off and over time, it developed a dirty line around the paint which I always wanted to remove.

A French door led to the garden with ledges either side. Above the sideboard was a bevel edged mirror, hanging from the picture rail. I would dust and polish everything as well as the picture-rail itself and skirting boards. The ornaments included a wooden fruit bowl, a couple of porcelain figures, and some glassware. Having been told that a good glass bowl made a lovely ring if you knocked it, I used to enjoy making it ring after I had polished it. Walking around the dining room used to make the crockery that was neatly stacked in the sideboard shake and emanate a distinctive rattle. We were always wary that it would all fall and break if we were too heavy footed.

After polishing everything, I would hoover and move onto the lounge.

The lounge was easier, only the TV, window ledge, small table and stereo/reel-to-reel tape recorder here and two speakers on the wall, along with two sets of plugs, picture rail, mirror and skirting boards. A few ornaments including a sea urchin, a few vases and a brass shell case decorated the room.

Into the hall and the wooden tea-trolley which was used as a table had 3 tiers and housed a brass ornament of the 3 wise monkeys, Mum's treasured royal Worcester lizard vase and a brass dish which we all put our car keys in.

The telephone in the hall sat on the painted box that housed electric and gas meters and above it was a small window upon which sat a porcelain Siamese cat. There was an electric convector heater at the bottom of the stairs which Dad regularly sprayed gold as the colour faded and bits of rust emerged. It was great in the winter when we were talking on the phone having the heater on, although time spent on the phone was limited because it was so expensive. We had to be considerate not just in our time spent using it calling out, but also care for those calling us too. If we wanted to have long conversations, we should go and see people!

Up the stairs and either side of the runner was painted white gloss, along with associated bits of dust that had landed in the fresh paint so caught the duster and grabbed bits of extra fluff.

The hoover reached most of the way up with the tools before it fell over and then had to be carried up to do the top few stairs. It was always a game to see how far up I could get before the hoover fell over.

The landing had an oak chest, a gift from a masonic 'do,' I believe, since my grandmother also had one. It had wooden mouldings on it and was a dust trap! It housed blankets, table linen and always smelt of 'clean washing' when you opened the lid. Before it took up post there, there was another cupboard which had a squeaky door, and housed all sorts of interesting goodies such as old photographs, and I remember an electric hand-held massager made from Bakelite. There were also evening gloves, fancy evening bags that belonged to Mum from her days of attending masonic ladies' evenings, or dances that she and Dad went to prior to having us children. In later years it was moved into the garage where it held stationery which all became old and a bit fusty over time but it was always neatly stacked and as the items were unused, we enjoyed looking inside it.

The bathroom was the next job. It housed a blue bathroom suite and black shiny tiles. I hated the tiles as they were a nightmare to clean. They smeared and left marks on them, and if you polished them, they left trails of rainbow coloured residue marks. No matter how much effort I put into them, they were never just plain black and shiny!

There was a small convector heater plugged into a socket in front of the toilet, and it resided between the toilet and wash hand basin. Despite all the later health and safety, we managed never to electrocute ourselves. Dad always said he couldn't understand what all the fuss was about, as there was just as much risk in the kitchen with water meeting electricity. I think he had a point and since we never tried pulling the heater into the bath with us, we all felt quite safe.

Behind the end of the bath was a space that Dad filled in and made into a laundry bin. Every week we would throw the contents down the stairs and gather it all up again for washing. I used to love throwing the washing down the stairs and it seemed a guilty pleasure of being reckless with intent. Mum always did it so I knew I wasn't going to get into trouble for following suit.

The window in front of the wash hand basin was frosted and used to get steamed up. Black mould would sometimes appear in the grooves of the wrinkled glass. I used to scrub it with a brush and watch the black water that ran down the glass with a pleasing sense of satisfaction.

Behind the bathroom door was the airing cupboard. The bottom housed the immersion heater tank with its bright red jacket and piled up next to it were packs of sanitary items and always a box of Lux soap flakes which Dad used in the bath. The toilet rolls were also kept in here. Izal! Scratchy, hard medicated and utterly useless paper which we all used for years until the advent of soft paper came along, although Dad still insisted on using hard paper for many years. The top cupboard housed bedlinen, towels and soap. As time progressed, Coal Tar was replaced with Lux, Camay or Zest. The carpet was a grey fleck and in years to come became quite thin. The problem was that because the bathroom was so small, and carpets came in 12 foot widths, Mum and Dad never got around to replacing it, because they felt the waste left over made the whole task too expensive. Once, when Mum and Dad went on holiday and Chris and I were left at home, we got so fed up with it we went to try and buy a new carpet and get it fitted during the week they were away, but failed since there wasn't enough time. We didn't realise it took 6 weeks to order and deliver so it remained as it was.

Last on the list of rooms to clean were the three bedrooms. Chris and I did our own so it meant only Mum and Dad's room which wasn't difficult with just a dressing table and side table to clean. The tops of the wardrobes had things on them so they didn't get done.

Although Chris and I shared a bedroom as small children, as we got older, Chris moved into the small bedroom. She took with her the more modern bedroom furniture comprising 2 chests of drawers and a wardrobe. I was left with the heavy oak furniture which comprised of a wardrobe, knee-hole dressing table and tall-boy. There was also another chest of drawers but both the tall-boy and chest of drawers were full of Mum and Dad's things including all the photographs. On top of the chest of drawers was a black and white portable TV, which we used to take to the caravan. It had a circular aerial on top but no matter how you twisted and turned it, it was always hit and miss as to whether you could get a picture and often once adjusted, as soon as you walked away from it, it went fuzzy. I never thought to switch it on in the bedroom. It was just there for convenient storage.

I also had a convector heater under a mirror on the chimney breast. On top of it was the ship lamp I loved so much and I had to remember to move it if the heater was on.

The carpet was a mustard colour with a swirly pattern on it. Made of nylon with a loop texture, it was very hard wearing and never seemed to look any different. If you dropped anything on it, it had an ability to grab hold of things and thread them through the loops and I can still remember the sound of breaking carpet as I pulled things like a dropped hairbrush from it. The occasional singe mark that happened from time to time, from the curling tongs landing on it for too long, were soon covered up by trimming the top off the loops.

In later years when I was leaving home, I remember having an argument with Dad as I started to pack up the curling tongs. He wanted me to pay for them since he said he had paid for them in the first place. They were several years old and I was so annoyed at his meanness, I told him he could keep them and I'd buy my own. Dad's hair was very thin on top and secured in place by Brylcream every day, so the possibility of him ever using curling tongs was nil!

Back downstairs and the kitchen was much easier to clean. A Formica table and a Hygena cabinet with a pull-down work-surface and which housed all the day-to-day items for cooking. Everything else went in the pantry and later when Savacentre appeared and we could do a monthly shop all in one go, we had an overflow cabinet in the second veranda.

For some reason the kettle was in the first veranda which attached to the kitchen, along with the fridge and tumble dryer. In the winter it was really cold going to make a cup of tea. We knew we were lucky to have a tumbler and getting the clothes out after a good swirl in it created so much static electricity it would make our hair stand on end., which was fun. This was life before fabric conditioners.

Considering the age we were, I don't think we did a bad job of learning how to look after the house although I remember a few incidents that brought Dad and me into conflict.

After Mum had died, one day Dad and I were in the kitchen and I was cooking tea. We were also having an argument. He accused me of not cleaning properly, citing the bathroom. Frogmarching me off to the bathroom he pointed at the cistern on the toilet. Between the lid and the wall was a spider's web. Ranting on at me he told me it had been there for weeks. I was furious. Partly because of his pettiness, partly because I thought if he had noticed it and bothered him so much, he should have done something about it, and also because I thought he was using the web as a monitor of my cleaning ability.

I was livid. I went mad at him and lost my temper screaming that if he had bothered to look properly, he would have seen that every week after I had cleaned, the web was missing. Clearly the spider came back and built a new one and I also told him if he was so bothered by it, instead of moaning and complaining he should move it himself. As I was in full flow, I took the tea towel from my shoulder and flicked it at the web with as much speed as befitted my anger.

All in slow motion, the lid of the cistern flew up into the air and crashed back down again. Amazingly, it didn't break. There was a stunned moment of silence and just as I turned away Dad smacked me really hard on the back. I turned and stared at him, said nothing and walked away.

It's the one and only time he hit me as an adult and I realise it was a boil over of anger and frustration, and I have to say I felt really pleased at having taken the moral high ground, I just walked away, which had the effect of making him feel really terrible. He had the good grace to apologise and we never mentioned it again.

The spider must have thought it safer to move house and was never seen again!

Ironically, in later life, Dad had a theory that no matter how long something was left untouched, dust only ever got so high. He said if you went to any derelict place, there was never more than a certain level of dust lying on things. I'm sure there's some law of physics to show this, as I have never seen it to be wrong. Shame he didn't apply it to home!

Church

As I said, I became really good at making gravy and Sunday roasts, although when I left home, I was so fed up of it, I rarely made any gravy or a Sunday roast for years. Sunday dinner seemed to take over the whole day, cooking it, eating it, washing up and then digesting it.

Mind you that wasn't such a bad thing in our early years, since Sundays were often extremely boring. As young children none of us were allowed out to play on Sundays for fear of upsetting either the neighbours or the good Lord, who rested on a Sunday.

Mum and Dad were both churchgoers in their younger days, but I wouldn't have described them as overly religious. We were brought up as Church of England, attended church occasionally and were taught to say 'The Lord's Prayer' when we were children. We believed the thunder was the Lord moving his furniture about and believed when we died, we went to heaven. We were christened, and had Godparents. We weren't taken to church every week though.

Dad apparently sung in the church choir when he was young and then played the church organ. No mean feat, our church had, well still does, have a beautiful organ. Oddly, we never heard my Dad sing. Mum was always singing and often whistling, and Dad would take the Mickey out of her. Consequently, Chris and I rarely sung in front of Dad in case he did the same to us, but we always had the radio on in the house during the day, and listened to music all the time too.

One tale we heard about Dad's organ playing was, ironically, when he was sacked! Apparently, he was practising one Sunday afternoon in the church on his own and decided to play something a bit more contemporary. Choosing to play 'Cruising down the river,' he was bought to an abrupt stop as unbeknown to dad, it transpired some people belonging to quite an eminent local family had arrived to visit the coffin containing one of their deceased relatives which was lying in the lady chapel. Unimpressed at being greeted to a recital of 'Cruising down the river' as they mourned their loss, Dad was removed from his post following pressure exerted upon the vicar.

As we got older, we started going to Sunday school at the local Methodist church. I don't really remember why, but I think it was to do with the fact that Chris joined the guides. I didn't join brownies or anything like that, but I remember going to Sunday school now and again, and then being in the Sunday School Anniversary, where we would all stand on a raised tiered stage and sing. Having rehearsed for a time leading up to the day, on the morning of the Anniversary, we would all meet at the church. David Harris had learnt to play the drums and he was in the boy's brigade band that marched in front of the parade, around the streets, providing music and drum beat to keep us all moving in time. It was a lovely day, and it was wonderful walking around the streets in the middle of the road with people coming out to wave to us all. I got a new dress and I was allowed to wear my silver cross, a christening present from my Godmother, and it all felt very special.

As the years passed, I no longer took part in the Anniversary or parade, but every year, they would march past our house which was on the route, and I would wave to David as he passed by playing his drum.

I was in the Anniversary and parade for a few years, and although I remember a few visits to the church, I don't remember many, so maybe they just needed children to make up the numbers once a year!

Sometime later, I was around 11, my sister and two friends, Sue and Jane, decided they wanted to go to church. As ever I tagged along with them. Sue always looked after me being a naturally caring and gentle girl, she always defended me when my sister was being mean to me. (40 odd years later, she still does!)

Chris made a big point of telling Mum and Dad, that if we went to church and didn't like it, or got fed up with it, we could leave going without them forcing us to keep going. They agreed.

Armed with a little book of The New Testament we got very good at reciting the Holy Communion, and singing hymns was something I really enjoyed. The sermon used to go straight over my head, I didn't really understand what the vicar was talking about, but going up to the communion rail to be blessed was very good and gave people a bit of time to chat as we all wandered back to the pews. Chris, Sue and Jane decided they wanted to be confirmed, so obviously I wanted to be confirmed too.

They applied to go for confirmation classes and were accepted, but I was told I was too young and the vicar refused to allow me to attend. Mum was really cross and pleaded with him to let me go with my sister and friends whilst showing an interest in it, but he was immovable.

I was really miffed to say the least and felt really out of it all. I vowed I would never be confirmed as a demonstration of my displeasure for his poor judgment, and in fact, I remained steadfast until I was 40.

Leading up to the girls' confirmation day, they were all bought a new outfit and given a little white handkerchief type head cover. I was in church

116

with Mum and Dad but very unhappy not to be in one of the starring roles. Going to church afterwards was never the same either. Going to receive communion also made me feel isolated as they all received the bread and wine, and I just got a pat on the head!

We joined the church youth club which met near the church and went there for a while, but eventually, we all got a bit fed up with it and decided to stop going to church. Chris told Mum and Dad we were going to stop going and it's one of the few times I remember Mum broke her word and told us we had to go. Chris, particularly protested, but Mum insisted we went. So, we did. Except that we would regularly play truant and sneak off to my nans house to drink milky coffee and have cake instead. She was sworn to secrecy and really enjoyed us going there for an hour or so until we could go back home again. Once or twice, Dad appeared and Chris and I would go upstairs to hide until he went.

Eventually, we stopped going to church and Sunday mornings were spent doing other things. For me often going to the riding school where I helped with catching the horses, grooming, feeding and generally helping out. They had up to around 70 horses at one time so there was always plenty to do.

Electricity and Sparks

Mum gave up work when she had Chris and me. She was a fantastic housewife and could make something out of nothing. She would sew, knit, bake, craft and also gave us lots of life-skills education. She taught us proper manners, how to play all sorts of games, and was always there when we got home from school. Something I treasure since her time with us was so tragically cut short. With Dad in charge of all our financial provisions, he worked hard.

Dad trained as an electrician, like his father before him. He went to the technical college rather than the grammar school and was a 'doer.' If you were in a tricky situation, Dad would get you out of it. He was clever and quick thinking and had a great sense of humour and mischief. In the adage of who would you want with you if you were stuck in the desert, it would definitely be Dad! He also sailed very close to the wind on occasions and that was something that could get him into trouble.

He used to tell us tales of the war years and doing National Service along with some of the mischief he got up to. Dad always described himself as lucky and he had some episodes in his life that supported this description.

One such occasion was when he was stationed at Shawbury Barracks near Shrewsbury. He wanted to go home for the weekend. He had a motor bike, but like everyone at the time, petrol was rationed and in scarce supply. Dad had what would loosely termed as a 'work around' plan. He stole it!

Petrol was dyed with red pigment on the barracks so that if it was stolen it could be identified easily and the offender punished. Dad had a couple of jerry cans and syphoned petrol from military vehicles as and when he could. He stored it in his jerry cans and then hid them under a bridge suspended by some ropes in a nearby river.

Deciding to go home, he took his bike to the bridge, topped up his tank and off home he went. Having spent a happy weekend at home he returned to Shawbury, but a mile from the barracks, he ran out of petrol. It was the first time he had misjudged how much petrol he needed and cursed himself as he had to get off and push his heavy bike the last mile to the barracks.

As he arrived on site, there was a huge kerfuffle going on. Dad asked what was happening and one of his pals said that someone had been hiding red petrol in jerry cans under the bridge and the authorities had found it and were testing everyone's vehicles to see who had stolen it. So far, none had been found but there were still people off site and they were waiting for them to come back. Dad breathed a sigh of relief and a gave a little prayer of thanks since when they came to test his tank, there was no petrol in it. Had he not misjudged the amount he needed he would have been caught and put on a charge.

Another time, he told us about a kit inspection. Every now and again, with no notice, the men were required to present themselves on parade with their kit bag. Kit had to be put in the bag in a particular way and folded neatly into shape to give the bag a proper shape. Dad, wasn't good at having a tidy kit bag. Folding wasn't one of his forte's. As the sergeant went along the line, the majority of men were told to open their bags and take out the contents. Dad had his stuffed with all sorts, but not kit, and not folded. As the sergeant went along, he stopped at Dad. Dad said he looked at him straight in the eyes and said he told him mentally to move along the line. After a few moments of meeting eyes, amazingly he did, and Dad escaped another charge.

As we grew up Dad did all sorts of mischievous things and never paid for anything that could be scrounged, begged, stolen or borrowed. It was part of the effect of the war. Make do and mend, none of the throw-away society that we have today.

Unfortunately, as my experience with Jess Maul showed, there were times when the consequence of these actions had a less than pleasing result.

Another was an episode Dad had with the tax man. Someone reported him as working and not declaring income. It was after Mum had died and Dad was under investigation. After much toing and froing, Dad went for an interview with them. Chris and I were worried that Dad was in serious trouble and that he might go to prison. For some reason the night before we had all been to church. Dad used to say that although he didn't go to church regularly, when he did go, he listened to the sermon the vicar delivered and in true lucky fashion, it came to be that this was his saviour.

During the interview, Dad was being asked about whether he was denying that he did any electrical work. He said he wasn't denying that and confirmed he did do some work.

The tax man interviewer then asked him about how much he earned from this work and Dad said he didn't earn anything.

The tax man asked, 'So are you saying you do this work for no reward?'

Dad, paused for a moment and remembering the sermon from the night before answered, 'The greatest reward any man can have, is contentment of the soul. And I have that!'

120

The interviewer was seemingly flummoxed by his answer and the interview was suspended. Nothing was ever heard from them again.

On the up side of the make-do-and-mend, waste-not-want-not attitude, there were many less stressful examples. Mum always used to swill a little water around the milk bottle and add it into the milk to make sure no milk was wasted by being left in the bottle. She used to wash out little plastic bags that food came in and hang them on the line to dry. They were then reused for food, sandwiches or to store other things. I remember the rustle of them blowing in the breeze.

Sheets were given a long and happy life, as they wore thin, they were either turned sides to middle, which involved the sheet being cut in half and resewn. With the two sides sewn together the previous middle piece ended up on the sides. It could be a bit uncomfortable lying on the seam, but we got used to it. Once the sheet had become too thin, it was then recycled into pillow cases. Once the pillow case had seen better days, the pillow case became a tea towel and after the tea towel had become past its best, it then became either a dishcloth or cleaning rag, before finally becoming a rag for Dad. Only then did it give up the ghost and become discarded.

Candlewick bedspreads were regularly dyed after fading in the light, and if blankets became too thin, they would be used as covers for furnishings during decorating. Emulsion paint was watered down to make it go further, although that was less effective as it did rather show in the finished effect!

Mum made all our clothes for many years and every garment had a hem with a generous turn up so that it could be let down as we grew taller. The visible line of the hem that emerged after turning down was covered by Ric-Rac or ribbon and where possible bias binding was used to cover the raw hem-edge for the last attempt to squeeze a little bit more length out of it. Being the smaller of the two of us children, I then got the cast offs from Chris as she grew out of her clothes. Sometimes this was good, if it was something I really liked, but it was a big of a drag if it was something I didn't like very much!

Invariably, she made us clothes that were identical and made out of the same fabric, but sometimes, as a contrast, they would be the same fabric but in different colours. More specifically, Chris's were made out of pink fabric and mine were blue. When Chris grew out of hers, I often loved wearing the pink version for a change.

As children we wore knee high socks or knitted tights. As we got older and grew too old to wear socks, we started wearing tights or stockings as was required with our school uniform. Choice was limited generally to American tan or black. Tights became more popular as an alternative to stockings, although they were relatively expensive and we regularly snagged them causing holes or ladders to form. We didn't just throw them out and buy new ones though, we learned to sew up the holes and ladders with cotton or nylon thread. Although it was a visible line they were nowhere near as fine denier as they are now, so no one took any notice. We also used to daub clear nail varnish over the ladder or hole to try to seal it and stop it running any further. We grew up with all sorts of these things, and never questioned it as it was 'just what we did.'

With Dad's practical skills, he taught us how to use a hammer, a screw driver, how to strip cable with a pair of pliers without cutting through the copper wire, how to wire a plug, change a fuse, change a tyre, check oil and water in the car, and all manner of generally male tasks.

For his ability to work for the reward of 'contentment of the soul,' I cannot remember how many ceiling roses I constructed for him, but it was fun.

One thing that he did for mischief involved a gadget that I always forget the name of. The trick he played on Christine and me only happened a couple of times because we became wise to it very quickly, but it didn't stop us joining in with it when he embroiled our unsuspecting friends.

It had its most magnificent application one day when very unusually, Dad welcomed lots of our friends into our garden to help fell a tree. It was a rather large and very lovely Rowan tree. As children we had a rope attached to it and we used to love hooking our feet into the loop and swinging around it, listening to the creak of the coir rope as we went. We climbed it, did somersaults on it and generally had lots of fun. In Autumn its lovely red berries would create a magnificent display. Mum taught us from an early age that these berries were poisonous so we were careful never to sample any to see if she was right!

At the end of the garden, we had several tall poplar trees. They formed a boundary between our garden and the house that backed onto us and were actually the property of the other house. The poplars were not only at the end of our garden, they extended to several properties next door to us and along the road. They were lovely and we watched birds come year on year to return to their nests and raise new chicks. Mum was an avid feeder of birds and any scraps of food were thrown onto the garden to feed the birds. When the wind blew through the trees, they produced a beautiful and relaxing rustling sound. We weren't so happy when the leaves dropped, but Mum would rake them up and set fire to them. She loved a good garden fire, but sometimes would start a fire when the leaves were a bit damp and one day created so much smoke, she sent me to go and check the traffic on the main road. She was right to feel anxious. The cars were all crawling along with their lights on trying to find their way through the fog of Mum's fire.

One winter night, the weather was very squally and next morning we woke up to see the smallest of the poplars lying flat along one of our neighbours' gardens. Its top leaves resting gently outside their French window. Until then, no one had really considered just how tall they were and what would happen if they fell. Had it not been the smallest poplar, it would have crashed through the roof of their house. All of a sudden, the beautiful poplars became a vision of fear. As it was cleared away it became apparent just how far the roots travelled and Dad discovered the reason our slabs were lifting slightly was due to some roots which were just a few feet from the foundations of the house. From then on, it was only a matter of time before all the trees had to be dealt with and the big Rowan tree was also doomed.

On the day of the tree felling, Dad invited all of us to dig around the bottom of the tree to expose the roots and start to dig them out. We had a great time. We all had our shovels, forks trowels and all manner of digging tools and in no time, things were going really well. Unfortunately, Dad developed a migraine and had to go and get some tablets and take a nap. He said it would be a few hours more before we got to pull the tree down. He had already secured some ropes around it for when the time came.

With Dad out of the driving seat we all got stuck into digging and as children couldn't wait to give the ropes a tug. We had several attempts with no effect so kept digging. When we couldn't resist the temptation to have another go, there was a lot of creaking and movement and the tree ceded to our persistence and started to lean. Spurred on by its movement, we pulled and dug some more and with one almighty effort, the tree gave up its foothold and crashed to the ground with a final crack.

We were thrilled and the noise of the crack woke Dad who came rushing out to be astonished at what we had done in the hour he had been asleep. In his usual manner he ran to get his camera to took a photo of us all standing on the fallen tree. Unfortunately, he forgot to put a film in the camera so we had to have a replay the following day! It's another photo that seems to have disappeared.

To round off a wonderful day, Dad got out his party trick! I think it was some kind of capacitor, but I can't be certain. I know it was a little square machine in a brown leather case. It had two wires coming out of it and he would give one to one person and one to another. He would then get us to hold hands and wind it up. After that, he would tell us to let go and whoever let go, would get some sort of static-type shock. As we had all our friends together, he got us all to stand in a circle and hold hands. He wound up the box and told us to let go of our hands. Chris and I were wise enough not to let go, but those who hadn't experienced Dad's machine before all let go and got a sharp bang as they did!

It probably all sounds very cruel and barbaric now and social services would have a field day, but in its day, it seemed it was just a bit of fun and no parents complained!

Dad being an electrician, he was also an electrical engineer and worked at various places during his working life. He worked for West Bromwich Corporation, later known as the Public Works department, nowadays, the council. He did some lovely things like install and maintain the sound systems in West Bromwich Gala Baths which were turned into a dance hall at various times, and he also did all the lighting for Dartmouth Park at various events. I had several photos of him on top of the roof of the iconic 'Threepenny Bit Café' that was in the middle of the park, and also climbing up several lampposts here and there. Unfortunately, the photos seem to have disappeared somewhere, so I can't show the proof!

Later in life Dad moved to work for the MEB, and at one time was responsible for street lighting. Dad would sometimes take us out in the car for a trip along a new road that was under construction or was being upgraded. I remember distinctly, being driven along the M5, and Newton Road in West Bromwich, when we were privileged to drive on a road that no-one else was allowed to. I admit to being underwhelmed by it all then, but can appreciate the idea of it now.

Another time, we were taken to a big set of traffic lights between Walsall and Lichfield. The lights were very tall, and we approached them along a very straight road that went up a bit of a hill.

Even I was quite impressed with these, they were apparently powered by phosphorus, or that was my understanding, they took a long time to get to full luminescence and made the traffic junction very safe at night. Even now on the rare occasions when I go past them, I remember seeing it all for the first time, and the regular times Dad would remind us of 'I did those lights!' I think he was quite proud of them.

I learned about how much distance there was between lampposts and the difference between urban lights and normal street lights and motorway lights.

I also learned how lights were distributed along a road. The lamppost directly opposite a road T junction was known as a 'stop lamp.' I learned that on a road with a bend, the lights are always on the outside of the bend, not on the inside, or either side, because of the way the light reflected across. In those days, which were before sensors, Dad always used to go and change the timer on the lamppost outside our house between daylight saving times as he had a key to the cover that housed the timer. We were very proud to have the only lamppost in the street that was in tune with the light and dark before the council came round to alter them.

My favourite story about my Dad and lampposts was one that involved him setting out a whole new set of lamps for a new housing estate. He had it all planned, drawn and set up. The lampposts were delivered and installed, but then the builder went into liquidation and the site was boarded up overnight. My memory was somewhere between Dad wanting to get his posts back as they hadn't been paid for, and the fact that somehow or other he might get into trouble, or have to account for how they were installed and not paid for. Either way, Dad decided he wanted his posts back, so in the dark evening, he persuaded a couple of the MEB workmen to go with him in a lorry and cherry-picker, and they went around the outside of the boarded-up site, and pulled up all the lampposts. Retrieved before the days of CCTV or site security, he was a happy man!

My final memory of a lamppost was in our garden! We had one that was chopped down in height and installed as a very sturdy washing line post. It was installed where the rowan tree had been. Painted grey, he also dug that one up when he moved house and took it with him!

During his efforts of extraction, he was using a big piece of angle iron to help raise the leverage of the jack that he was using. Such was the security of the lamppost foundation, it all slipped and the angle iron hit my sister on the head. Although this would normally be something to be very concerning, at that time, my sister was suffering from optical neuropathy, which was a precursor of MS, and she had lost the sight in her one eye. The blow to the head had the effect of restoring her vision. So, it was all a win-win as Dad got his lamppost and Chris got her eyesight back.

I'm sure all the rules and regulations have changed, but I regularly think of Dad in relation to street lighting.

Captain Pugwash & UK Travels

We were lucky enough to have two TV sets when they were black and white. When we had a colour set, of course we didn't really want to watch anything in black and white, so it seemed we often all sat in front of the colour TV together. No video recordings, catch-up or play on demand, if you missed the programme, that was just tough luck. With only 3 channels, and no one really liked BBC2 much, it was down to two choices. People would talk about whatever the most popular programme had been the night before. and eagerly anticipated storylines and plots that were upcoming.

After Mum died, TV watching wasn't the same. Dad was often in his shed prior to losing Mum anyway and only came in for News at Ten, which makes the idea of Dad and me watching something together very unlikely, especially when it happened to be Captain Pugwash!

Captain Pugwash was a cartoon and was on between 5.35 and 5.40 immediately before the evening news. It was really silly, but Dad and I used to laugh our heads off at it.

I was telling someone about this story on the day I wrote about it and was told about the double meanings of Captain Pugwash so thanks to the wonder of Wikipedia I looked it up and it seems a lot of it was urban myth. I can't remember anything other than it was an innocent pleasure that Dad and I both enjoyed watching.

Another programme we really enjoyed watching together was 'Joe 90.' A super clever, young, boy puppet who regularly saved the world from some deadly disaster. Whilst Dad and I enjoyed these two programmes together, Chris was rather the opposite and her TV watching with Dad was 'World at War.' I found it depressing and scary. Just hearing the sound of the music was so foreboding along with the narrator who was so mournful, that I would go off to leave them to it. Even now, the sound of the music is enough to make me turn it off. So, I was Captain Pugwash and Chris was World at War. Speaks volumes really!

Several programmes we enjoyed as a family, as did lots of our friends, including 'Morecambe and Wise,' and 'The Generation Game,' with Bruce Forsyth and his array of beauties including Anthea Redfern. It was a must watch and we learned lots of things watching the various games that people had to try to do. At the end of the show, the winning pair got to watch a series of items going past on a conveyer belt and if they remembered them all afterwards, they got to take them home. We girls all really wanted to go on and win a fondue set or a hostess trolley, which was the height of luxury dinner party entertaining, not to mention the ever-present huge cuddly toy!

Chris and I also used to love watching Top of the Pops on a Thursday, as did our friends.

When we were small, I remember watching Cilla Black and Lulu and lots of other 60's stars often perform on TV shows. Chris and I would stand on the window ledge behind our bedroom curtains and appear from behind to sing a song. I would be pretend to be Cilla and Chris would be Lulu.

When I was really young, I thought all the people on TV lived in the back of it and came out onto the screen when it was their turn. I used to look behind to see if I could see them!

Since the TV wasn't available to watch 24/7 as it is now, we used to listen to the radio a lot. We all loved music and I still do. I feel blessed to have had parents who loved all manner of music from many genres and I have a wide repertoire of music to listen to, much of which would appear to emanate from well before my time. We also liked to listen to radio programmes and during Saturday lunchtimes we would listen to 'Jimmy Clitheroe and the Clitheroe Kid' together. At the caravan for many years all we had was a radio and we enjoyed listening to all manner of programmes. 'Sing Something Simple,' 'Family Favourites,' the BBC world service programme, for British people in the forces, who would send messages and requests for their loved ones, as well as 'Friday Night Is Music Night.' 'Ed Stewpot Stewart' and 'Tony Blackburn with his dog Arthur' were particular favourites and it was several years before I learned that Arthur wasn't a real St Bernard who sat in the studio! In between all these programmes, the shipping forecast used to be regularly updated and for many years, I could recount all the shipping areas around the UK. In recent times, Chris relearned them, so I did the same!

As Mum and Dad had both lived through the second world war, anything to do with wartime was a must watch. Lots of films were made and the tunes that signalled which film we were about to watch were also listened to on the record player. Haunting music that was as strong as the message of war. Mum and Dad were understandably keen to visit museums that housed any sort of relics of the war, and I remember especially 'The Colditz Exhibition' at the Imperial War Museum, which had some amazing and ingenious artefacts that people had used to secrete maps and all sorts of paraphernalia, in all manner of things. The one that struck me was the heel of a shoe that slid backwards to reveal a secret space in which a tiny map was hidden. This was many years before James Bond had one! I remember Mum had a little book in our bookcase about escape stories from Colditz. We read it now and again, but I don't think I realised how true they were until the TV series about Colditz was aired. It was another must watch and we were amazed at the inventiveness of how they tried to escape from the seemingly inescapable castle.

During our childhood, we visited a huge array of castles, stately homes, museums, air-shows and any other events or places Mum and Dad felt worthy of a visit. With nothing much to entertain us on Sunday's, TV being non-existent until Songs of Praise at tea-time, and then everything that followed it, like 'Upstairs, Downstairs,' being very sedate and befitting of the Sabbath, we now know we were very lucky to be taken to so many places, although on occasions Chris and I felt very stately home, museum and castled 'out!' Some of them were very underwhelming and the rooms seemed to all look the same. Cold, stark, full of ancient artefacts that we couldn't touch and worn-out carpets. I couldn't wait until we could go outdoors and I could run around and explore. Dad was never far away with his camera and cine camera, which often brought us back to behaving and standing like little soldiers and statues as we were told to do this, that or the other. Most of the cine films involved us walking slowly towards him and the camera trying to look natural. It never did, but it did provide a visual record of all the places we went to. Unfortunately, at the time of writing, the cine films seem to have disappeared and no-one knows where they ended up, which is a real shame. The only record of them is from when Dad decided he wasn't going to pay the price to have them transferred professionally to video tape, so just filmed the cine films projected onto a screen, with a more modern camera. The quality really isn't very good, but it's better than nothing.

Although I enjoyed the outdoors, I found some of the air shows a trial, as not only were they always cold and draughty, the noise of the aircraft passing overhead was deafening and used to make my ears ring for days. It was only many years later in adulthood, when I realised I had tinnitus and my hearing was very sensitive, that hardly surprisingly, the worst aircraft that affected me was the Vulcan Bomber. As I write, it's been recently decommissioned and spent a year touring the UK. I can't say I was keen to go and wave a fond farewell. Having felt the thunderous noise and the ground shake, as well as how it made my chest vibrate as it rumbled ominously overhead, flying low across the airfields at the various air-shows we attended as children, I was happy to keep that one consigned to memory.

The Red Arrows were a different story, as they did amazing aerobatics leaving patterned trails of red, white and blue smoke in their wake. When I was quite small, I wasn't very fearful of things and I remember at one show watching a lady wing-walking on a bi-plane. As the plane made several turns across the field in front of the watching crowd, I couldn't understand what she was doing that was so impressive. From my perspective, she certainly wasn't walking on the wings, she was just strapped into a frame and waving at people. I didn't think that took much courage.

Nowadays, I simply can't imagine being strapped to a metal frame and being dragged through the air several hundred feet above the ground, with nothing but a bit of strapping to keep me in place! Funny how perceptions change as we grow older and our heads become filled with endless possibilities of things that can go wrong. Lack of faith in equipment is very sobering. The same happened with the parachute jump I always wanted to do as a child. Now I would need a bucket full of Valium and some very strong pants, along with someone pushing me to get me to jump out of an aeroplane.

One place we did enjoy visiting was Downing Street. In those days there was only a policeman outside number 10 Downing Street and anyone could walk up and down and linger and peer into the windows as much as you wanted to. I distinctly remember, Mum, Chris and I walking along arm in arm together, looking into one of the basement rooms and noticing it was piled high with boxes and boxes of toilet rolls, as Dad filmed us on cine camera. We found it amusing that they seemed to have the need for so much of it, and weren't impolite enough to comment on the reasons that most people would assume these days!

Another place we liked to visit was Stonehenge. Again, in those days, there were no restrictions on where you could go, so we used to take a picnic and sit on the stones, running between them playing all sorts of games together, before waiting for the sun to set behind the Heald Stone. From there we would sometimes go to Old Sarum, which was, and still is one of my most favourite places. At the time we used to go, it had been tidied up and the outline of the ruins were lined with flint. In between, lay beautiful, green, spongy grass, and Chris and I would have carte-blanche to run around freely. Most of our visits were just for a day, so involved several hours in the car, although in those days, it was very rare to be stuck in a traffic jam.

We visited London often. Mum and Dad had some family friends, Uncle Ben and Auntie Dorothy, as they were known to us, who lived in London and always made us welcome to stay there. Uncle Ben, would sometimes come with us into London to show us where to go, how to get there and enjoy the places we visited. The only problem was both he and his lovely, kindly wife were also serious tea drinkers. It seemed before we could do anything we had to have several cups of stand-your-spoon-strength very bitter tea. Wherever we went and Uncle Ben was with us, he wanted to drink tea at regular intervals and Dad used to get very agitated as it slowed down our planned journeys. It was always met with an overly generous 'never mind,' if Uncle Ben couldn't come.

It meant we visited almost every museum in London at that time, as well as seeing all the famous, and not so famous sights. One day we took a wrong turn and ended up in the middle of Horseguards parade. Another time we found ourselves in the atrium of the Home Office! Both very imposing and no one there to shoo us away.

Sometimes, we would go to London just for the day. In those days parking wasn't a problem and we even parked outside The Houses of Parliament one Sunday so we could have a wander around and take some photos. We went to visit HMS Belfast, which was an unexpected pleasure as we imagined what it was like for the seamen who had lived and worked on board. Some of the small shared cabins and hammocks we saw made us realise it wasn't a glamourous life on board. The photos failed to meet their mark on this occasion, as the camera door wasn't shut properly so all the photos came out with a faded glow down the one side. It mattered not as we had a really good time without them.

An exhibition I really enjoyed was the Apollo moon landing exhibition. I think it was Apollo 11, but don't quote me. We watched the first, and subsequent moon landings on TV as so many people did and it was all very fascinating. Looking into the night sky and imagining people walking on the moon was awe inspiring. Seeing the little scorched capsule that looked no bigger that a small funny shaped disc, was incredible. How on earth it made it safely back to earth is a wonder to behold. We also saw some moonrock. It was a very small fragment, housed on a big glass case, held gently by a little metal grasp and it turned gently and slowly around. It was a big surprise that it was actually black, and we were educated that the little silvery bits that sparkled within the black rock was what gave the moon it's silvery glow that we see here on Earth. We saw the astronaut's suit, which looked less than comfortable, and the whole exhibition was a joy to see. I was very lucky to have the opportunity to go back to see it with a school trip sometime later. I was so excited, I remember being on the coach and telling my school-friends all about it before we got there. I must have seemed a proper little know-all!

One we missed though, was the Tutankhamen exhibition. We were going and actually arrived to see it. It was only on tour for a short time and the queue to get in was enormous. Dad decided he didn't want to wait in a two-hour queue so we left. We heard lots of spooky tales about people who met some sort of mysterious fate after viewing some of the artefacts during its tour, so I was pleased not to have been.

Another unexpectedly pleasing museum, was Bovington Tank Museum in Dorset. We were allowed to climb over a tank that was outside the exhibition and of course Dad had his camera with him. Inside the exhibition, there were lots of scary looking tanks and armoured vehicles. The one that fascinated me most was a tank that could throw out fire and burn everything in front of it, along with one that had chains that would be flung out ahead via a turning roller which would blow up land mines in advance of the tank.

One particular favourite was Hampton Court Palace. I remember the astronomical clock which fascinated me beyond measure. It just seemed to do everything possible and I remember Mum explaining it all to us. We saw the 'real tennis' courts that were still in use and I remember the gardens being wonderful, as well as the old grape vine which was over 200 years old. There was also one particular huge beautiful tree standing majestically seemingly on its own, nothing to impede its growth and canopy and I could imagine a big swing on it. It's one place I want to go back to.

We All Go Flying

When we were young, Mum and Dad bought us a kite. It was a blue box kite and it didn't matter how much wind was blowing, which was rarely a problem on the north Yorkshire coast, it was completely unflyable. Mum and Dad would take it in turns to run up and down the beach with it, and as Chris and I got older, we would try to make it fly too. Although we were bought a new kite which did fly, it remained an endearing challenge to see if anyone could get the box kite to fly. It never did!

Dad on the other hand wanted to learn to fly properly in a light aircraft. He didn't have normal hobbies, like our friends fathers, Dad's hobbies were definitely outdoors and one day, he had the funds to do it. It started with a one-hour flight from Bobbington in a Cessna light aeroplane in Stourbridge where he got to go up with an instructor, take hold of the controls for a little while, and that was it. He was hooked! He booked some lessons and every week on a Saturday we would look heavenwards to see how high the cloud was to determine if it was a good flying day or not.

Dad soon learned that it was actually better to move his lessons from Bobbington to Elmdon, as it was in those days, now Birmingham airport. The facilities were better and it was cheaper. I remember it costing £17.50 an hour at one point which seems unbelievable compared to what it must cost now. It wasn't a cheap hobby, but he enjoyed it and for probably the first time in his life, he was interested in books, well, they were actually 'how to fly' books! He studied them and then had to take exams to progress to the next level.

As he was learning, he regularly told us we were very lucky to be able to go with him and sit in the back seats of the little aeroplane and enjoy the ride as he did various tasks as part of his tuition. I have to be honest, I never felt lucky when it was my turn to go and Dad used to get crotchety with me because I wasn't gushing with a great desire to go.

I appreciate that for some people, it would be an unexpected pleasure to be able to go up in a small aeroplane, but with all the noise, draughts, and in my opinion, lunatic father in charge of the controls, it wasn't my idea of fun or pleasure!

Dad was a terrible map-reader, and as I mentioned before, an undiagnosed dyslexic. Putting him in a light aircraft with the controls wasn't my idea of fun and the only thing that ever made me feel lucky was either not having to go, or reaching terra-firma in one piece. Admittedly, until he passed his exams and obtained his full pilot's licence, he wasn't allowed to take passengers unaccompanied, so we always had a fully trained pilot with us, but

Dad was always at the controls as we wobbled, dropped into air pockets and did steep turns and stalls as part of his training. Dad had an idea that once he passed his test, he could take us all to France for a couple of days with him at the controls.

When I say steep turns, I mean they were the sort that made the ground appear at your side, and unfortunately, I had learned enough about flying that if they were too steep, you could drop out of the sky. The other thing was stalling. This involved taking the aeroplane up to a point where the propeller was pointing towards heaven, then stalling the engine. Following this, as the now silent aircraft fell backwards towards the ground, it was somehow be tipped forwards and downwards somehow and the engine would restart. I was petrified! And as if once wasn't enough, we then got the pleasure of doing it all again! Christine on the other hand seemed to lap it all up and went with Dad regularly.

There was one exception to this horror for me, and that was a day when we went up on a grey day and were enveloped by a big layer of misty cloud. As we climbed higher and higher, we suddenly ended up in a breakthrough and below us was an endless, unbroken vision of fluffy, white, cotton-wool clouds and above us a crystal-clear blue sky with big ball of burning sun shining down upon us. It was a day to remember and having never experienced flying apart from with Dad, it was an image that filled my heart with joy and wonder. I also felt extraordinarily safe as I couldn't imagine falling through the cloud. It just looked like a big springy base. It was the one and only time I felt safe in the plane.

As if I needed proof of my lack of faith in Dad's flying ability, he provided several stories to prove me right. One of them I was 'lucky' enough to experience with him.

We took off and everything seemed fine. As we were coming back, the heater failed and apparently, it meant the engine was in danger of freezing. Thankfully, I wasn't aware of how dangerous this was, but the end result was, that Dad got priority landing, all the big aircraft were sent away to fly around in circles for a while and we were accompanied alongside the runway by a fleet of fire engines.

His next brush with danger was when he was flying on his own. The engine cowling came loose and again, the engine was in danger of freezing. For a second time, Dad was accompanied along the runway by the fleet of fire engines. The problem was made worse as Dad had bought a short-wave radio and tuned it into the channel he was using so that we could listen to him as he flew around and communicated with the tower. Mum was listening in and was dreadfully upset, made worse as it was during a time when she was quite poorly and in a very fragile state. She sometimes went with him, but when he was on his own after that, she didn't like listening in to the radio and never settled until he was back down safely.

Probably his worst near miss, was one day when he was having a lesson and thankfully, no-one apart from his instructor was with him. As part of the licence requirements at that time was the need to be able to recover the aeroplane from a spin. In order to do this, he needed to get it into a spin, which I believe involved stalling as previously described and at some point, tipping the wing in one direction and as the plane was freefalling in a spin, push the nose to restart the engine and recover from the spin. Just writing it down sounds like some sort of aeronautical Russian roulette and with Dad in the pilot seat, that was bound to be a problem.

Apparently, when the 'G' force hits your body, you can blackout as the blood is forced from your head, during the recovery the 'G' force works the other way and you 'red out' which means you blackout seeing red, (well who wouldn't see red in a stalled spinning plane,) as the blood rushes back into your head. The result was that Dad passed out temporarily and as he did so, the instructor tried to take over the controls but Dad's foot was stuck under the rudder pedal and meant the instructor couldn't reverse the spin. (If you are a pilot reading this and I have some of the details mixed up a bit, please forgive me,) but essentially, they were heading for the ground in a nose dive. Luckily for both of them that Dad managed to come around and somehow move his foot at around 1500 feet and live to fly another day. The instructor landed the plane safely and they both fell out of the plane very shaken and stirred, to which they took a very necessary whisky to restore their nerves. It must have been bad as Dad didn't drink much at the best of times, and never touched strong spirits. Thankfully, Mum wasn't listening to the radio so was blissfully unaware of his latest brush with mortality.

As he progressed with his training, he started flying solo and had to navigate his way to other places and build up his flying hours. One bright day he decided he would fly to Bristol airport, land and have a break before returning to Birmingham again.

He got his maps out with which he had to plot his course. They were laminated and he used to use a big black waxy pencil to chart his course which could then be removed before planning the next journey. It all looked very impressive until he had to apply the map plotting to actually flying the route.

Amazingly he got there. He told us that light aircraft flying relied a lot on seeing what was on the ground. He knew the motorway network well so followed the M5 down to Bristol, turned left near the Severn estuary and somehow found a big runway which was Bristol Airport.

Pleased with himself, he had a cup of tea, used the bathroom facilities and headed back home.

Using the same skills as he found the Severn estuary, he turned right and followed the M5 all the way back to Birmingham. By the time he got to Birmingham though it was starting to get dark and the motorways and main roads all had the lights on. Dad got confused by it all and ended up lost. Fuel was running down, but eventually saw a lovely long straight line of lights and started his descent to land. Thankfully, he realised early enough it wasn't quite right and was able to abort the decision to land as he discovered that he was heading down to land onto the A38. Running beyond the emergency fuel and nearly on fumes, he rediscovered his bearings and managed to follow the road network again and make his way over to the airport landing safely.

Occasionally, he would have a very uneventful flight and often would fly over to West Bromwich and over the house. Friends and neighbours would go out into their gardens to wave at him, and Mum would hang sheets over the washing line so that Dad could identify more easily where we lived. His camera at the ready, he would point it out of the window and take photographs of our house, and surrounding area. Sometimes he did it flying solo and occasionally, some poor unfortunate friend or other would volunteer to go with him. I went a few times if I couldn't think of any reason not to, and whilst the memories of the traumatic experiences have now mellowed, I have to say though that I believe West Bromwich was a lot safer when Dad stopped flying!

Sometime later as we got to late teens, my Godmother's husband arranged for a group of us to go gliding at Cosford. When we arrived, there were two gliders, one closed in and sleek looking, and one open top and looked a bit like an old, green, upturned rowing boat. Guess which one I went in? Correct, the green one. Dad's idea and to be honest it was the right decision. The sleek one involved sitting behind the pilot tandem-style and looking out and around. The open topped one was sitting side-by-side to the pilot and feeling the wind blow through my hair was an experience. As the pilot found out I had been flying quite a lot with Dad, he handed me the controls to have a go at steering the glider. I felt infinitely safer in the glider than the plane. With no engine and simple rudder controls, I had much more faith in physics than I did with Dad. It restored my faith in flying.

Gadgets

Dad loved gadgets. He loved to fiddle with things, find out how they worked, fix things and make do and mend. He was a bit of a hoarder as many people of his generation were. The war years meant making the best of what you could get your hands on and being creative. Dad retained this skill, although some things worked out better than others.

Being dyslexic, Dad didn't read instructions, he worked it out. One day, he went shopping to get a new spin dryer. He parked the car in the multi-story car park in West Bromwich and went into the shopping centre. Whilst he was in the shop, he spotted a new gadget. An electric tin opener. He couldn't resist it and so along with the spin dryer also bought the can opener.

He carried the rather heavy and cumbersome boxes back to the car park and to where he thought he had left the car, but couldn't find it.

Assuming he was on the wrong floor, he went to a different level and couldn't find it there either. He went to various floors and still it eluded him. Part of the problem was that he didn't know the registration number, just the colour and make. Tired, fed-up and weary arms from carrying his packages, eventually he found an abandoned shopping trolley, pushed it to the top floor and came down each level walking around the whole floor before finally finding his car. This was before automatic electronic keys, something he would have found very useful!

Home with his goodies, he unpacked them and tried out the spin-dryer first. Filling it with wet washing he switched it on and watched it take off across the floor. He rearranged the washing and tried again. Same thing happened so he packed it all back up again, put it in the car and drove back. This time he noted where he parked. In the shop he told them it didn't work and took it out of the box to demonstrate. Chris had a school-friend who worked in the shop and he was serving Dad.

'Did you read the unpacking instructions?' he asks Dad.

'No, but I know how to use a spin-dryer.' replies Dad.

'So, you know you need to remove the packing bolts?'

'Ah…' says Dad. 'I forgot about those!'

At least he knew where the car was and by the end of the day we had a fully functioning spin-dryer and new state-of-the-art electric can opener.

Dad couldn't wait to test the can opener and was thrilled with it. Over the next 3 weeks we opened more cans, but something wasn't right. The cans weren't being opened properly, they were wonky and ragged and all in all the cans weren't opened properly. The cutting wheel on the can opener was all chewed and mangled. Dad realised the metal of the can opener was softer than the cans and had warped and twisted. Flabbergasted by the fundamental design fault, he was on a mission. He got all his mangled tins, put them in a two carrier bags and along with the can-opener set off back to the shop. Arriving in there, Chris's friend was unluckily the assistant Dad found first. He found a plug and set up the can-opener. Tipping the cans out, and turning them upside down, he started demonstrating the inadequacies of the gadget. Unfortunately, he hadn't bothered to wash the cans first so you can imagine the unpleasantness of it all. He was surprised that the staff weren't as overwhelmed by the failings of the design flaw, but was impressed with their speedy response to replace it or give him a refund. He decided it might be a one off and swapped it.

The assistant said, 'don't worry if it does the same as the other one, just bring it back. We won't need to see the tins, we trust you!'

Back in school, Chris was suitably embarrassed as they told the tale about Dad. Thankfully it wasn't in an English lesson in front of 30 other people as had been my experience.

The second one was also not up to the job and he took it back, minus the cans, but sometime later when it had been redesigned, he persevered and bought another one. It was still going strong when my stepmother, Heather died in 2019!

One of the most wondrous gadgets was when dad came home one day with a little Casio calculator. I remember the four of us crowded around as he pushed the buttons and showed us how it added, subtracted, multiplied and divided at the mere press of a few buttons. It also did percentages and square roots which was marvellous. I remember he told us it cost £24, which was a large amount of money then, but we all thought it was well worth it, and although we take it all for granted now, I am still in awe of the technology it entailed.

A Saturday Job

When I was about 14, my friends and I all wanted a Saturday job. In those days, we had a school uniform and day to day clothes, but other clothes were often things we had for Christmas or birthdays. The nearest we got to designer was an Adidas or Gola bag for the boys, and in later years, we were all allowed to wear an Adidas T shirt in PE. Green Flash pumps were the height of fashion for sports, and for day wear, we girls all wore crepe-soled lace-up shoes courtesy of Freeman, Hardy and Willis. For the summer, we all had 'Jesus sandals' which were very flat and buckled. Even our mothers were surprised by the ugliness of them, but fashion is a funny animal, and as they were good for our feet, our mothers happily bought them for us.

Once we moved on from them, we all went to Dolcis for the latest platforms and then the very high, very large platformed 'blocks' which were only for the really chic amongst us. Mum was horrified when she saw them and I was persuaded, as in, 'no you can't have any blocks,' to have a pair of strappy, wedge sandals with a much smaller platform.

So, if we wanted other unnecessary frippery, we needed to work and provide it for ourselves. We all trawled the town shops for jobs, but we weren't allowed to work in them. We needed a national insurance number and those weren't given to us until we were 16.

We were allowed to have a paper round and also work for up to 5 hours a week under 16. That wasn't much good to us, so we all just lied about our age and got a job in the indoor market.

There were lots of stalls but those that had the most young staff were the fruit and veg stalls. Evans had about 3 stalls and lots of staff and despite asking there every week, we couldn't get a job. The other one was Paul Marsh. He only had one stall and one Saturday, he said he had a couple of jobs going so we could work there. We were so excited! We started at 8.30am and finished at 5pm. We earned £2.50 for the day and after some time, we were given a raise to £3 and then £3.50.

At the end of a long Saturday, we would run all through the town to try and get to Chelsea Girl boutique before it closed, to see if we could afford the latest 'whatever' to add to our wardrobes.

I loved working on the market stall. It greatly improved my maths as we had to do calculations and multiplication by mental arithmetic. We got so good at it, we could be given numbers and know the answer without having to work it out.

We learned that tomatoes were a fruit, not a vegetable, and that sprouts were far better after the frost had caught them. In the winter it was so cold, we wore fingerless gloves to help keep our hands warm. Even though it was an indoor market the fruit and veg were so cold to touch as they were often still coated in ice.

As time progressed, we often had opportunities to work extra hours as the adult staff took time off or left. We worked hard and by the time we came to eventually leave, the number of staff had fallen from 13 on any one day, to 6 or seven.

Even though it was obvious to everyone else that our employer must have known we were underage, we never knew, and so having practiced our dates of birth regularly in case he asked, from time to time we used to get spooked that he would ask us for our national insurance number and we would all have to leave. He never did.

After a couple of years on the market I was 16 and my sister, who had been working at Littlewoods, put my name down to work there and after a time, I was called for an interview. I got the job and so with a sad heart, I left the lovely fruit and veg stall. The money was far better at Littlewoods so it wasn't a difficult decision although given the same money, I would probably have stayed.

I started on textiles and this also included wool. I was taught another life skill here in how to fold clothes shop-style. I found wool rather boring as people bought it, then put-by some spare to make sure they could get more of the same dye number. It all seemed to get complicated as the cupboards underneath became crammed with noisy scratchy plastic bags of oddments of wool and I could never seem to find the one that the customer wanted.

Another thing I struggled with on textiles were the tills. Great big electronic things, and each product had to be entered with a different coded button. Instead of being labelled 'wool, men's, women's, children's, hats,' etc, they all had a department number. Working only one day a week, to begin with I couldn't remember the numbers and I was regularly in trouble with the snooty head of department for pressing the wrong buttons. If someone bought items from different departments, all hell let loose as I pressed all sorts of wrong buttons. Then adding up was done by pressing other buttons and if you got it wrong, it involved Miss Snooty coming to adjust the till and having to make a report about an 'over-press,' (Invariable) under-press, (rare!) or mis-press, (also invariable). I really needed a flow chart to tell me which buttons to press and in which order.

One Saturday morning, we had only just opened and a man came in to buy lots of lovely presents for his wife for Christmas. He was my first customer and I put all the goods through and then pressed the wrong button, which then doubled the amount of his bill.

Too scared to ask Miss Snooty to amend it, I just blagged it and charged the poor man double. He looked a little surprised by the size of the bill, and was probably too embarrassed to complain at how much he had spent, so just paid. I still remember it came to £32 instead of £18! I have always felt guilty about it, but it probably saved me being sacked. Hopefully he realised later and took it back when I wasn't there!

I was feeling very unhappy and wished I was back on the fruit and veg stall, when one day in the canteen, I was talking to someone and they suggested I ask for a move onto food. This sounded much more me, so I did. After 6 weeks, and some repetitive asking, I got a move and next thing I am on the cooked meats and pies counter.

I loved it. Most of the staff who worked on Saturday's were part time, young Saturday staff and we all got on well. I was amazed how much people bought and especially the sausage and brisket. It flew off the shelf and we were replenished regularly by the young man in the cooked meats prep room. Depending on how much we needed, sometimes he would bring it all down, and other times we would go up and just get an odd tray or two. Leaving the shop floor was something of a treat and a privilege for those of us working on the meat counter, as every other time we wanted to leave the floor we had to ask permission from a supervisor or one of the store managers.

Opposite the cooked meat was the sweet stand and more especially, the chocolate coated Brazil's. They were enormous, and very delicious. We were forbidden to eat on the shop floor and were not allowed to eat any of the goods. The temptation of the chocolate Brazil's was too much for most people and as they were so expensive, we couldn't really afford to buy them. We had to find another way, so invariably, upstairs, tucked away around a corner, was a big plastic bag of chocolate Brazil's, with a little hole in the bag. Put your hand down the back and you could just about extract one. We didn't have pockets in our tunics so there was no chance of hiding them there, so the only option was to shove it straight into your mouth! Then began a challenge of eating it before someone caught you. They were so big, it was a trial to get it all under control and swallowed without being seen, but the reward of it was well worth the risk.

Transformed by the pleasure of being very busy and working with nice people, I loved working here. Occasionally, I would do a stint on the cheese counter and got really good cutting cheese with a cheese wire, something me sister wasn't so good at. Although she had left by now, she used to get into all sorts of trouble for breaking too many cheese wires!

I then used to go onto the tills as people brought their baskets of food goodies through. These tills were great, easy to use, no complicated department buttons and they were really fast. They restored my confidence in my till-skills, and I used to try and get things through as fast as possible. I remember one day, being so quick, the food was flying down the packing chute and as the customer handed me the money his hand got a bit too close to my till drawer. In my haste, I nearly took his fingers off as I slammed the drawer shut! These days I would have done really well working in Aldi!

The Pyrex Bowl

When Mum was still well and able, she continued to run the house. Although he was very practical Dad didn't cope with it all very well emotionally, and every now and again there would be a trauma. Chris seemed to be able to keep out of the way but I was more challenging towards what to me seemed like unreasonable behaviour. He was moody and could be spiteful, but I didn't realise that at the time.

One evening I had been out at my friend's house. She lived around the corner and I used to go there a lot. It was always more relaxed there. I came home and rang the doorbell. Dad came to the door and was having a right tantrum. He had been helping Mum to wash up and had been drying a Pyrex bowl. As I rang the doorbell, he dropped the bowl and it broke. He started shouting at me for it all being my fault and that if I had been back earlier, he wouldn't have dropped the bowl.

I was furious again. I felt the injustice of blaming me for his accident was so unfair and of all the arguments we had over the years, this is one incident I still feel was outrageous on his part. Mum tried to smooth it all out but I was having none of it and refused to have any blame apportioned to me for simply ringing the doorbell.

The other incident, which was for me the worst thing he ever did, was sometime later. Again, Mum was still alive, but very poorly.

I had been out with my boyfriend for the evening. It was a winter evening and cold. He had walked me home and I invited him in for a cup of tea before he walked back.

Dad wasn't happy about any of it. He didn't like me having a boyfriend let alone bring him into the house. I made the tea and went to sit in the dining room and drink it. It wasn't very late, but Dad was evil. He came into the dining room and summoned me out. Taking me into the second veranda he started having a go at me. He was venomous. I could only hear the fire and spit coming from his mouth as he verbally assaulted me. Thankfully, I can't remember exactly what he said, but he did make out that it was my fault Mum was going to die because I had brought someone home. I was so distraught and unable to cope, I shrank down into a crouched position and realised afterwards I had been pulling my hair out as my hands were covered in it. He could see my absolute distress and continued to be horrible and irrational to me. When he eventually finished, I went back into the dining room and my boyfriend was gripping the arms of the chair like a vice. He hadn't heard every word but knew Dad was being horrid.

I don't feel the need to forgive my Dad for this. It was his culpa not mine, so I refused to adopt it in any way. He was totally unreasonable and it was the worst thing he ever did in my eyes. I remember wondering how he could ever have been so cruel to accuse me in any way of being responsible for my mother's impending death, and whilst I appreciate we all say things we don't mean when upset and angry, this one is something I would never ever think, let alone say. I didn't speak to him for days afterwards and did my best to avoid even seeing him, leaving for work very early, and coming home after he had gone to bed.

I knew he was being totally unreasonable, and although I was terribly upset, I also knew it was his overreaction to a traumatic time. That didn't mean I let him off the hook. Understanding it, didn't make it acceptable.

Exams

At the end of the 5th year of Menzies we are all getting prepared to take our exams. In those days, it was either 'O' level or 'CSE.' If you weren't deemed clever enough to do an 'O' level, you were entered for the seemingly lower-level exam of CSE. If you were successful in attaining a grade 1 CSE, it was considered equivalent to an 'O' level grade 3.

I was taking Geography, Chemistry, Social Economics, Commerce, Home Economics, French, English and Maths. All but French were 'O' level, French was CSE.

I wasn't very good at revising. I had no idea how to do it. We were encouraged to attend after school, extra lessons to be guided by our subject teachers, but along with a general teachers strike, which meant that many of them were working to rule and after school activities were not to be undertaken, it really didn't really sink in very well. I found generally, I either knew it, or I didn't. Lots of things had no context to my daily life and this is something I still struggle with as an adult. If I am learning a new subject but have no reference to apply it to, it all just seems to float about in the air with nothing concrete to attach it to.

My friend Jackie had no such problems. What she sometimes lacked in common-sense and an ability to work something out with practical, daily living skills, she more than made up for, with her photographic memory. I was very envious of her ability to do this. Whilst we were both in the top set for subjects, (apart from French), we were in separate classes, but with the subject content being the same, we were able to revise together.

I have a love-hate relationship with multiple choice too. You get a question, try and work out the answer before reading the choices, and then because they are out of context with anything, I can instantly find a good reason for all of them to be right, and can be wholly relied upon to pick the wrong one!

Maths wasn't a strong subject either. We learned to use a slide rule and logarithms and we learned all sorts of wonderful theories to work out how far it was from the corner of one side of a triangle to another. In the exam though all of this abandoned me and I remember having to work out the height of a circular cone which had had the top cut off. All I could do was use a ruler to extend the side lines upwards until the crossed and measure it. I know I got the right answer, as we talked about it later, but I didn't show the calculation I used, so would have lost marks for that.

Describing how an Ox-Bow lake was formed or glaciation for geography was much easier. It involved a visual image and physics so I could easily do that. I also remember distinctly understanding how an artesian well worked and how water could be drawn up thorough an Archimedean screw.

During revision, I was asked to describe it verbally once by John Parkes and one of the other geography teachers, as they asked me, 'How does an Archimedean screw?'

'An Archimedean screw is for drawing water. It is a big tube with screw in the middle of it and when turned rapidly it forces water to be drawn up through the middle and out through the top.' I couldn't understand why everyone laughed at the time, but with hindsight I discovered it sounded rather rude! (Maybe I got extra marks for that description!) They used to test me regularly on it to make sure I had learned it well, and every time, they giggled!

English literature was surprisingly difficult. I felt as though my imaginative brain wasn't beyond primary school level and as for Shakespeare and critiquing books, I found it all a bit boring. Poetry did nothing for me at all. Just a lot of words that often didn't rhyme, with an underlying meaning that escaped me.

I enjoyed reading 'Animal Farm,' but didn't get it was about anything other than some farm animals having a bossy leader. I read 'To Kill A Mockingbird,' but only saw it was a sin to kill a mockingbird, and some man was defending another man and he was very unpopular for doing it. 'Julius Caesar,' well, he had a bad day in March and was betrayed by his friend Brutus. And as for, 'As I Walked Out One Midsummer Morning,' I couldn't get that at all. I was confused that someone would just walk out of their house one day and go on a trip. It all sounded a bit reckless!

I was better at English language, or so I thought. I could write a brilliant envelope, where the address, (in those days) had to be written at a perfect 45-degree slant and you had to be able to line it all up against a ruler, and I knew how to write a letter, with appropriate signing off, yours sincerely, faithfully, or whatever, depending on how you started it. However, during my English language exam, I managed to turn my paper upside-down midway and started writing from the back. Then at the end, I realised I had missed out one question completely, and unsurprisingly I failed the exam spectacularly with the worst possible outcome which was a 'U.' Unclassified!

Exceptions To Prove A Rule

One story that I still remember embarrassingly was at an end of year celebration at School. Instead of the normal end of year disco, the 6th form students were going to do a very new and posh thing by going on a River boat shuffle. It involved chartering a double decker bus, driving about 25 miles to the River Severn at Stourport-On-Severn, dancing the night away on large boat whilst cruising along the river and then returning back again. I was invited with my boyfriend and had bought a new dress for the occasion.

I was very excited and nervous, but the weather was lovely and off we went. Arriving there, I was asked what I wanted to drink. I hadn't got a clue, but heard a girl ask for martini and lemonade, so I said the same. It was horrible! I tasted it and it made me pull a face, so after a while, I thought the best thing to do was knock it all back in one go to get rid of it when no-one was looking. Asked what I would like later, I heard someone ask for Cinzano and lemonade so I asked for that. Equally disgusting, again I knocked it back after a time and next time I had lager.

I wasn't used to alcohol, even less I had no idea not to mix drinks and especially with a long drive back on a bus. Added to this less than elegant cocktail was the fact that drinking and driving wasn't an offence then, common sense was the rule. However, our bus driver had enjoyed the evening as much as we had and got on the motorway going south instead of north, so the journey was not only much longer than it should have been, it was a bit uncomfortable as we weaved our way home.

Knowing my previous problems with travel sickness, you can imagine what happened next. My stomach evacuated the contents of the cocktail all over the bus. I can still visualise the full horror of it now (although I'm sure you can imagine the scene) as I wanted to disappear in a hole.

To be fair, I wasn't the only person to feel very squiffy, as none of us were drinkers in those days, and no-one said anything to me, but my embarrassment was further aided as we eventually got off the bus and my boyfriend said, 'Do you mind if I don't kiss you goodnight?' Needless to say, I didn't, and I'm amazed I ever saw him again!

My next experience of excess alcohol was at my Godmother's house celebrating her daughter Liz's 18th Birthday. I had worked all day in Littlewoods and somehow missed eating lunch. I had a quick tea and changed, then went to the party. They lived in the next street so only a couple of minutes away. They had bought a big keg of cider and Liz's Dad was keen to empty it so that he could reuse it for his homebrew. Neither I, nor most people, ever got to the end of the glass as it was filled up at every possible moment. Consequently, I had no idea how much I had drunk.

At least this time I recognised feeling queasy in time to get to the toilet, but was apparently gone some time.

Going home later, I found it very difficult to get the key in the front door lock as it seemed to keep moving around and there seemed to be two to choose from. Deciding that I didn't like this feeling it was a very long time before I had any alcohol again.

A few years later, at a 21st birthday party I was very pleased with myself having found a lovely non-alcoholic drink. I went home and Mum was still up. Telling her all about the evening, I effused all about the lovely drink. Mum asked what it was called and I told her it was Pernod and blackcurrant. Mum went pale. 'That's alcohol,' she said.

'No, it isn't alcoholic Mum, it's like blackcurrant and liquorice.'

'Pernod is alcoholic' she said. 'How many did you have?'

'Seven! But it isn't alcoholic.'

Mum nearly choked. 'It's very alcoholic! You had better get to bed, you will have a terrible head tomorrow.'

I was still unconvinced. I couldn't believe something so nice could contain alcohol. I went to bed and slept like a baby. Waking the next morning, Mum came to see how I was and was amazed that I was absolutely fine. No hangover or after effects and I was still convinced Mum had got it wrong!

Although we didn't drink alcohol very much, there was a fashion for home brew and my sister Chris decided she wanted to make wine. She bought all the equipment and made several demi-johns of red wine. We watched it all ferment for many weeks and eventually she decided it was ready to bottle. Having spent hours sterilising, corking and labelling the bottles, she laid it down under the chest of drawers in her bedroom where there was a handy gap and pretty much forgot about it, until one week, when she kept hearing strange noises. Eventually, she discovered the wine hadn't actually stopped fermenting and was blowing the corks out, spilling the wine all over the carpet. We managed to clear it all up and rescue some of the bottles although I don't remember actually drinking any of it!

6th Form

At the end of our fifth year at Menzies, exams were over and we had to make a decision what to do for the rest of our lives. We had a careers advisor who was also a teacher and her main aim seemed to be to get us all to work in a factory. One day there was a flurry of excitement as she had been offered the opportunity for two jobs being made available to work as prescription pricing administrators. I had no idea what this entailed but it made me realise we were all about to hit the real world of work and I didn't feel ready for that yet!

My sister had stayed on at school into the 6th form so I did the same. Having been a prefect in my 5th year, I was also elected Vice House-Captain too. As I began the 6th form, I was elected girls House Captain for Trojan. I also got a new tie for being awarded my senior house colours. If only I could have been so successful in academic studies.

The start of a new year, and as 6th formers, we were given a bit more leeway and a bigger opportunity for self-responsibility as we were now able to enter the inner sanctum of 'The 6th Form Common Room.' We didn't have to wear a uniform all the time either and us girls were also allowed, for the first time in our senior school life, to wear trousers! Whilst the novelty of this made us feel a little bit smug, we often chose to wear our uniforms including tie, just because we wanted to show that even if we didn't have to wear a uniform, we still could. After 5 years of trying to wear our uniforms in a way that challenged authority, where we would try to assert our own form of identity and included things like leaving the top button of our shirts open, ties worn at various lengths and tighter or looser than was allowed, as well as the wrong colour of blue uniform and wrong length of skirt, now we couldn't wait to put it all on properly. Talk about reverse psychology!

Another of our smug pleasures was that no-one other than the 6th formers and teaching staff were allowed into the common room, which made it an altogether attractive place for the lower school to hang around. We had a kitchenette and comfy chairs. At break times we could go to the common room to chat and feel smug that we could now avoid getting wet and cold.

There were a few rules though and one was that we weren't allowed in the common room during lesson times. If we had 'free periods' which were properly known as 'study periods,' we were told we had to go to the library and do some private study. We had a very good library complete with librarian, but of course, spending time in there when we could have been having fun elsewhere was intensely boring as we had to sit in silence.

So, we cheated. We hung about in the common room instead, but the deputy head at the time, Mr Basset, was determined we would obey the rules. He was a very 'old school' type of man with a grammar school sense of authority and obedience. Very stern with no sense of humour, he looked extremely old-fashioned and wore squeaky shoes. He was not a man to be meddled with. Every now and again, he would appear in the common room and throw us out to go and study in the library. We would walk around the block a couple of times and then wander back again. He became more and more annoyed and we were threatened with detention or having the privilege of the common room removed. We ignored this and continued to flout the rule and wander back again. Mr Bassett got wise to this and hatched himself a plan.

There were two entrances to the common room, one from the outside and one via a room from the music block. One day he came and threw us out and unbeknown to us, went around the other way and lay in wait in the music block. Aided and abetted by the equally strict headmistress, Miss Booth, he waited until we all wandered back and then reappeared.

We scattered, but our headmistress appeared via the other entrance and we were trapped. I remember a group of us girls ending up in the toilets and after considering climbing out of a window, eventually, came out as the headmistress, Miss Booth came in.

Mr Bassett did the same in the boy's toilets and after emptying all the cubicles, there was still one remaining with an occupant. Mr Bassett was not going to be defeated, and in an act as out of character as if the Queen had scratched her bum in public, Mr Bassett climbed onto the toilet in the adjacent cubicle and hauled himself up to where he could peer over the top and looked down.

'Kirk, what are you doing boy?' he boomed.

Young Kirk looked up, completely unperturbed and replied, 'Having a shit sir.'

Mr Bassett coughed and spluttered as he lowered himself away saying in a rather less booming tone, 'Oh, well, right, well… just hurry up about it boy!'

Yes, sir. Anything else sir?

No, carry on Kirk.

Thank you, sir.

You can imagine just how much fun we had with this knowledge and for a while afterwards, Mr Bassett left us alone!

The subjects that I had decided to study for 'A' levels were geography, economics and we all had to do general studies. I have absolutely no idea what general studies involved and I can't even remember going to any lessons about it, so it couldn't have been very interesting.

I liked economics and we were given a wine-coloured hard-bound exercise book to write in. That felt very grand. I learned about supply and demand curves and the stock exchange and we were able to take part in a virtual inter-school game where we were given a certain amount of money to 'buy' shares and each week we could 'buy' and 'sell' them. The competition was to see who could make the most money, or lose the least. We didn't win and were eliminated within a few weeks. We learned about banking and cheques and all sorts of useful life skills relating to the financial world we were about to join.

My favourite things of all though, remained the extra-curricular activities of sport and inter-house competitions.

One day I came home from school and Mum said, 'I think it's time you got a job. You aren't really interested in the lessons and are just messing about with everything else.' She handed me the Evening Mail newspaper and said 'they are recruiting for the civil service, why don't you apply.'

I felt later that she wanted to make sure I had a job and was settled before she died.

Starting Work

Chris was already working for the court service at West Bromwich County Court and so it seemed appropriate for me to apply to the civil service too. I filled in an application form and posted it off.

Very soon I had a reply and an interview at Five Ways Tower in Birmingham. Situated just off Five Ways Island, in its day, the tower was like something from a sci-fi movie. Red brick and black glass windows, it was very futuristic looking. Dad took me and I remember getting into the lift and being whisked to a high floor so fast, I felt my stomach lurch and my head swim. I felt so important being in this wonderful building.

I had an interview with 3 people behind a table who asked me all sorts of questions some of which were about my interests and hobbies and I remember telling them I enjoyed sport. It felt more like a chat than an interview and in no time, I was being hurtled back down to the ground floor as my stomach and head whirled in the opposite direction.

A few weeks passed and I had a letter arrive. I had been successful and was invited to join the DHSS. Department of Health and Social Security at Parham House, West Bromwich to start on 21st April 1980.

And so it was, that on 28th March 1980, as we broke up for Easter, with mixed feelings I left the 6th form of Menzies and all the fun and friends I had there, to move into the big wide world of work.

The two weeks of Easter after leaving school passed quickly, and quite a few of us from school met one day to go swimming at West Bromwich Gala baths. We had a lovely time there and at some point, I dived in head first into the deep end, misjudged the depth and bumped my head on the bottom of the pool. No harm done but I ended up with a black eye and followed that up with burning my neck with the curling tongues sometime later. This meant I started work with a black eye and what looked like a nasty love-bite on my neck!

It didn't seem to make any difference as I wore a high neck jumper, lowered my fringe and put some make up on.

The first day went by in no time. I was introduced to another girl who was starting the same day, and the training officer. After about an hour, she announced it was time for breakfast and we were led to the top floor and into the canteen. There was a queue of people and two elderly ladies behind a counter cooking in a large kitchen. Talk about Little and Large, they were so opposite in every sense. We found out later the larger lady who bounced around with a heaving cleavage was affectionately known as 'Slop' based on

153

her preparation and delivery of food. She was also in charge. The other lady Nellie, was a kindly lady who was constantly being told off by Slop for getting things wrong and not performing in the way Slop wanted her too.

Slop came up with the most amazing concoctions of food and nothing anyone asked for was impossible. Chip and marmalade sandwiches, chip and cheese sandwiches, in fact chip and anything sandwiches, but mornings were proper breakfast foods with bacon, eggs, sausages, mushrooms and tomatoes on bread or toast being the most popular. I discovered that as I was under 18, I was entitled to meal tokens. I collected them from the finance office and could use them to get free food. In those days I could eat whatever I wanted to and never put any weight on so I regularly had toasted bacon sandwiches. I was amazed that staff could leave their desk to go to get food and be paid for doing it!

The lady who was our training instructor was very kind, and she knew the rule book off by heart. In those days the rule book consisted of two A5 sized binders called the 'A' Code. It held all the information needed for us to assess claims for supplementary benefit, or 'supp ben' as it was referred to. This was for people who were out of work and had no income. I had no idea at that time what social security was let alone supplementary benefit. I soon learned it must have been important as we were taken into the secure room of the finance office and had to sign the Official Secrets Act. In exchange we were given a yellow plastic folder which contained the rules of our employment. It all felt very serious and we felt very important. We were told that if we ever left the civil service, we had to hand in the rule book so we must look after it with the utmost care.

We were given 12 weeks training in the training room and at the end of it we had to go on a residential five-day course to Preston. The only thing was that as I was under 18, I couldn't go, so would have to wait until after my 18th birthday. Everyone seemed to relish the idea of going away to Preston and we were also given a subsistence allowance for going. The week was to teach us how to interview people when they made a claim for benefit. In those days everyone who made a claim for benefit had to have a personal one to one interview. It was something else I wasn't able to do until I was 18.

The other girl who was training with me was a bit older than me, so could do everything earlier, but she was really good fun and we became good friends.

After 12 weeks in the training room, we had passed our initial training and were allocated to a section. This consisted of one of 6 sections each with 4 clerical officers, CO's, one clerical assistant CA, and a supervisor, EO. 3

154

clerical officers on each section had an allocated alphabetical split of the alphabet known as a box split. My section was H-K and I was given I-Ka, the fourth person was known as the 'spare.'

Every day, a selection of people would go to the post room and open the daily post. There was a particular way of opening things which ensured all the envelopes were opened fully, post sorted for various areas of the office and the envelopes were then rechecked for items that could have been missed. The clerical assistants would then be tasked with 'linking' the post to the relevant 'case paper.' At that point they would be deposited on our desks for us to action the post.

The CAs were amazing. Their knowledge of where every single case paper was in the office was superb. They often knew where each other's cases were too. No mean feat when there were so many different areas of the office the cases could be.

Live and dormant files, desks, book room, NO5 officer, finance, visits, LR, overpayments, URO, SCO, direct payments, HEO's room for checking, and at various times of the year, uprating, and this was all spread over various floors of the office. They then had to take the cases from place to place.

Occasionally, a casepaper would go missing and no-one could find it. On these occasions, we would have a 'stop' which involved the whole of supp ben not being allowed to move a case paper and everyone had to stop and search an allocated area for the missing file. Often it was misfiled, or had slipped behind a drawer or had been mixed-up with other files. Families or people who lived in the same house were all linked together with coloured tags and travelled around the office together. Thinking back, I wonder how I ever learned how it worked!

I felt very proud after my 12 weeks of training to be given my own desk with drawers, my own phone, 'box,' which was my alphabetical allocation of work, and stationery. That was all great until the phone rang and I had no idea what to say or how to deal with the question! The same applied to the post that arrived attached to the casepapers. It was all very well in the training room, but in real life I hadn't a clue what to do!

As an example, one day I had a phone call and a man on the end of the phone told me he was 'on the box.' I had absolutely no idea what he meant. He said he'd sent his box note in and wanted to know where his money was. I asked him to hold the line, whilst I asked my section colleagues what 'the box' was. They told me it meant he was sick and the box note was a sick note from the doctor. I learned that this meant the box was a reference to a coffin, so being on the box was sick whereas being in the box was being dead. It was a new language.

Never mind, I wasn't the first trainee and like lots of others before me, I was assigned a mentor. Her name was June. She was indomitable, came from Lancashire, had a bosom that had more support than a Sherman tank and she scared the living daylights out of me. She was there to help me through my probation period. It felt more of a prison sentence sometimes as she seemed to think she could explain something to me once and I would understand. She was wrong!

I lost count of how often June would tell me something and I hadn't a clue the next time it came up and it didn't help that she was so uncompromising and never seemed to crack her face into a smile. I would build up the courage to ask and she would reply in exasperated tones, 'Oh, but I've already shown you that!' June would then turn to Gerry, my supervisor, and peering over the top of her glasses, announce, 'Gerry, I've shown her how to do this and now she's asking me again!'

I discovered however, that June held a soft spot in her heart for me, and wanted to mother me. On my 18th birthday she presented me with a plain silver bangle. It was really kind of her and I wore it regularly. Unfortunately, it used to clang on the desk all the time so I stopped wearing it at work. June noticed and quizzed me about it so I told her I was worried about damaging it at work and kept it for going out. She was placated.

She also felt the need to protect me from the regular Friday lunchtime pub trip. Hard to imagine nowadays, but people regularly went drinking on Friday lunchtimes, or any other day for that matter. It wasn't against the rules, and if it was someone's birthday it was obligatory! June didn't approve and although I didn't want to go much in any case, she made sure I was aware it was very much frowned upon by her.

College

Like lots of things growing up, whatever Chris did, I followed. Sometimes by choice, sometimes just because it was expected. After Chris started work, she was allowed day release to go to college and do a qualification. It was an HND. It was said to be equivalent to 'A' levels, but one day a week and subjects were more business related.

Once I started work, I was given the same opportunity. The civil service used to allow people to do all sorts of courses of education and pay for them. People regularly studied all sorts of random subjects, paid by the government and then left to pursue careers in whatever it was, very often nothing to do with anything that was relevant to the job we did! Eventually, the government realised it wasn't the idea of it all and tightened up on it. I imagine these days it doesn't happen at all.

So, as a new civil servant. I was offered a day release place at college. I didn't really want to go, but was told by Dad it was an opportunity I should take and be grateful for, so I enrolled and on Tuesdays I was given the day away from work to go to college. It was meant to be one full day and one evening. For me this turned out to be one whole day, 9am to 9pm as my evening period was the same as my day one. Dad dropped me off and picked me up.

I hated it!

From the first day I arrived, I knew it wasn't for me. There was nothing about it that interested me, and having spent all my years at school with people I'd grown up with, teachers who knew us all so well, arriving at a cold harsh-looking building full of people I didn't know, with subjects I hadn't the faintest interest in, it was awful. I wanted to leave. I told Mum and Dad I didn't like it, but Dad insisted I went. Mum wasn't well enough to intervene, so it became a stand-off between me and Dad. Hard to imagine, I know! Every Tuesday Dad and I would argue and fight about me going and he insisted I went. I cried every Monday night, and didn't understand a word of what I was supposed to be learning when I got there. I resisted buying any books as they were really expensive and I knew I wasn't going to complete the course. I just hadn't figured out how I was going to escape. Being fair to my young self, I genuinely found it difficult what with learning all I needed to know with a new job, then taking a day out of the week and losing the continuation of my working week. The work I did was something that couldn't be left for a day, so I had June covering my work on Tuesdays. I had then lost the thread of everything and found it disruptive to get back into again. Being fair to Dad, he

157

probably though it was a good thing to do, but I still can't understand how he didn't see how the experience of it was affecting me so profoundly.

I remember one day it was lunch-time, I went to the phone box nearby and phoned a friend, I can't remember who it was, but I was so unhappy I was sobbing on the phone. Distracted when I left the phone box, I realised fifteen minutes later, I'd left my purse behind with around £30 inside. When I went back, unsurprisingly it was gone. It just added to my misery. At that particular time in my life, I couldn't remember ever being more miserable.

I confessed to my supervisor that I was really unhappy with college, and she told me to leave. I explained about Dad being so insistent that I go and said I should be grateful of the opportunity. Thankfully she realised just how much I didn't want to go and came up with a plan. At the end of the first term, she arranged for one of the senior managers to write a letter asking how I was getting on at college and telling me I didn't need to go if I didn't want to, that it wouldn't affect my job or career prospects and that I should only continue if I wanted to.

Taking it home to Dad, he relented and allowed me to leave. I was really surprised since he had been so adamant about me going. My relief was immeasurable. I'd managed to escape with only buying one book, the cheapest one of all of them. Going back to work and being there five days a week was wonderful and I've never regretted my decision.

Learning To Drive

When my sister was 17, Dad took her out in the car and taught her to drive. She failed her first test for driving too slowly, which was a bit of a surprise, as we all thought it would be her three-point turn that would let her down.

She learned to drive in the Morris Oxford. It was a big car in its day and power-assisted steering didn't exist, so turning the wheel was hard work and difficult. We watched her one day as she was practicing her three-point turn and in the effort of not overhanging the pavement ended up doing a 13 point turn. We gave her a round of applause when she had completed it.

Of course, when I was 17, it was my turn and although I was keen to learn, Dad took it all very seriously and I felt rather frogmarched into the car. The first lesson wasn't too bad as we got onto a main road and did only left-hand turns going around a loop several times. At the end of the lesson I hadn't stalled, hit anything or anyone and apart from Dad saying I was going around corners too fast it was all rather pleasant.

After that, it became a regular trip out in the car as he attempted to teach me to drive. By now I had another boyfriend and often I would drive there at the end of the lesson, Dad would drop me off and drive home.

One day we were having an argument. I was in floods of tears but still driving. Amazingly, we continued to drive and practice three-point turns, reverse around corners all whilst arguing and driving. I can't remember what it was particularly about but at one point he accused me of my boyfriend being 'the be all and end all of my life.' I responded with, 'well, Mum is yours.' His answer was 'no, she isn't.'

I was so astounded I managed to reverse into a newly planted tree and it seemed to break the tension as we drove away and I was dropped at my boyfriend's house. I'm not sure whether he meant it or not, but there seemed no point in my answering or commenting.

In between all this, Dad used to take my sister and me to work most mornings and when Chris was learning, she would drive, and when I was learning, I would drive. By now the Morris Oxford had gone and Dad had a company car. First a Vauxhall Viva, then a Morris Marina, and finally a Morris Ital and despite its shortcomings in many areas, the Ital had the best heater of any car I can ever remember.

Another time we were driving and it was a time we weren't actually arguing, but I got very confused turning right onto a dual carriageway and ended up on the wrong side of the dual carriageway, facing the wrong direction. Amazingly Dad was very calm in such situations and just helped me steer the car back to the right direction and carriageway.

Having studied The Highway Code, I was ready to take my first test. I say first as it ended up taking me three attempts to pass. My failures were because of the following.

My first failure was due to my confusion of knowing my left and right. The instructor told me to turn right at the end of the road, but I turned left. He pointed out my error and despite my limp attempt to say I thought he said left, I failed. I was peeved as the week before I had done most of the driving as we went on a last family holiday back to Bridlington. I drove up hill and down dale including Rosedale Bank and felt very confident. I parked and reversed easily and felt very comfortable behind the wheel.

The second test I believe was partly to do with the fact that I was rather overwrought and tired. Mum had had a bad night and at this time we used to take it in turns with Dad to get up to help her and I had been up eight times. I failed for misjudging where the end of a road was and braked rather sharply as the 'T' junction appeared in front of me sooner than I expected.

Dad was as disappointed as I was. He wondered if it was his teaching and so paid for me to have a few lessons before my third test which I thankfully passed. I don't think it was anything to do with my paid lessons or any inadequacy of Dad's teaching, as although we didn't see eye to eye a lot of the time, his driving teaching skills were very good and I passed my test two days after my 18th birthday, a few weeks after Mum died.

Having learned to drive, I wanted to have a car. To begin with Chris and I were allowed to use Mum's car, a blue Vauxhall Viva. Mum wasn't the best driver in the world, she learned to drive when the driving test didn't exist and was a nervous driver. Dad was much better but used to drive everywhere at a snail's pace. Tootling along, we used to say, letting the other cars overtake and have the stress. This was fine on holiday with nowhere to go and all day to get there, but there were times when we wanted to get to places a bit quicker. Part of the speed was determined by the fact that it was much more cost efficient to drive slowly. Dad didn't have to pay for petrol in later years as it came with the car, but only if he was filling up at work, so we used to travel everywhere with a few gallons of petrol in plastic containers in the boot so that he could fill up free of charge. The smell of petrol seeped through into the car as some of the containers weren't designed for petrol carriage. He also used to use petrol for cleaning marks off the carpet at home and you can imagine what that smelt like and how long it lingered! It's amazing we survived without any explosions.

Later, when I had my own car, he would give me a gallon or two free of charge from time to time, but more likely he would 'sell' some of his 'acquired' petrol to me to save me money on buying it! Win-win then, he got money from me for stealing petrol and I got cheap petrol.

He reckoned he had the most efficient car in the fleet as he would siphon off some petrol and store it for later use. The mechanics at work were always tweaking the engine to make sure it was running as efficiently as possible and Dad had to make sure his car was seen as doing a reasonable number of miles per gallon with the petrol he was putting in it. In order to do it, he often wrote down the miles we travelled and the amount of petrol used.

Not long after I passed my test, I was going out one day to visit a friend. The handbrake on Mum's car was dreadful. It needed fixing, as did the clutch which was also dodgy.

Mix the two together with an inexperienced driver, and you can guess, a problem emerges.

I reversed the car gently out of the garage down the drive which was on a slope, and ever so gracefully stalled. Twice. On the third occasion I heard and felt a crunch as the car slid into the side of the wall which fronted our house.

I got out and saw the car was stuck to the wall by the wheel arch. Rather than do more damage, I went in the house and told Dad 'I've got the car stuck on the wall.'

Amazingly, he didn't get cross and came down to help me get the car off the wall. With a hammer and chisel to remove some bricks, and then with him driving and me lifting the wheel arch, the car freed itself. Waiting for the eruption that didn't happen, he handed me the keys told me to go and drive, and said it was his fault for not getting the car done. I was flabbergasted!

Fair do's to him though, as I was a nervous wreck driving. I expect had he not sent me out, I think we both knew I might never have got back behind the wheel again.

After a time of driving Mum's car though, Dad started complaining about me using it too much and I knew more than anything it was because it allowed me unlimited freedom to go out especially if it happened to be a boyfriend, so after another argument and trauma, I decided to buy my own car.

Midland bank were advertising on TV as being the 'listening bank' and encouraging people to go and see them if they wanted a loan. In those days you only got a loan after being interviewed by the bank manager who had total discretion as to whether he (rarely 'she') would grant you a loan. Often people were turned down so would lie about what they wanted the money for and then worry that they would have to prove to the bank manager that the money had been used for the purpose it was granted. I booked an appointment with the bank manager and applied for a loan to buy a car which was granted. I had £1,000 and it would take me 2 years to pay back.

Dad wouldn't have anything to do with my car buying and so I was on my own. A man at work said he would come with me to look at cars and I settled on a bright orange Chrysler sunbeam. WOE 968T. WOE being the clue here, it became a bit of a challenge.

I brought the car home and Dad told me I wasn't allowed to park it outside the house. Yes, I know it was the Queen's highway, and I paid my car tax and insurance, but it was enough trauma having it, and I wasn't up for another challenge and argument as to my citizen's rights just then, so I started off parking it around the corner in the next street. Eventually, his curiosity got the better of him and he 'allowed' me to bring it into our street, but parked up the road. Only sometime later did he allow me to park it outside the house and then, all of a sudden, my car was accepted as he found it extremely useful to load it with rubbish for the tip or for moving heavy and large items around since it was a hatchback with an easy access boot space.

To be honest, it wasn't a bad car, but had an aluminium engine head which I discovered meant they were prone to warping, twisting, overheating and breaking. The temperature gauge used to fly up towards the red if I was in queueing traffic and eventually, I had to take it to a garage to have the radiator repaired... several times... in fact, so many times that I saw the kitten they had at the garage grow into a full-size cat! They tried taking the thermostat out which helped, but meant the internal heater didn't work which was very unpleasant in the winter. They were great people though and very kind to me and eventually gave me a new radiator free of charge.

One trauma sorted but another began as I could now drive myself to work and regularly take my sister. After a time, Dad told Chris she had to give me some money towards petrol, Chris wasn't keen since for her I was going that way anyway, so not using any more petrol than travelling alone. Dad kept on at her so rather than give in, Chris started travelling by bus rather than give me any money she didn't feel I was entitled to. I felt awful, stuck between a rock and a hard place it seemed even when Dad was standing up for me, it still created tension. Fortunately, we got past that one too and it seemed somehow, I had cast my independence to own my own car. Ironically, my owning my own car meant that Mum's car became very underused so sometime later Dad offered to sell it to me as it was sitting in the garage doing nothing. Chris rarely used it, so eventually I sold my orange Sunbeam and took over ownership of the Viva.

We often forget these days just how temperamental cars were back then, and in relative terms it wasn't that long ago. The boys usually learned how to solve problems with cars and did all sorts of things to maintain and improve them. Most of us girls hadn't a clue really, managing to fill up the water bottle, check the oil and for some of us, change a tyre.

The Viva was a special car. Lovely to drive, but temperamental about the weather, it was fine as long as it was kept in the dry garage, but if it was outside, including being at the end of a workday, and the weather was warm and damp, it was a nightmare to start.

You had only one chance, which involved an elaborate process of pulling out the choke fully, gently putting the accelerator to the floor, then turning the key and praying it would fire.

Regularly this failed, and if it did, you could be there for ages trying to get it going. The best way then was to leave trying until the petrol had evaporated and then start again. Sometimes in winter, it was easier to get a bus to work.

Funnily enough it also started to develop problems with the radiator. Someone once helpfully checked the water in the radiator and changed the radiator cap. I'm convinced the extra pressure caused by the new radiator cap, upset the whole balance of the cooling system and the temperature gauge started to increase. I found if you tapped the gauge, the needle dropped down and for months this seemed to work! Yes, I know that's rubbish, but it was easier than admitting the radiator was overheating.

Eventually it all got too much and the engine died on the M5 motorway. Fortunately, I was near the end of a service station slip road and managed to limp up the ramp. Someone came to my rescue and towed me all the way home from near Bridgewater. Thankfully the motorway was quiet, no one stopped us and despite being very cold, (no heater) and no servo-assisted brakes, (hard to brake!) I made it home safely. The pistons were reground and the engine rebuilt, but I never felt comfortable driving it again.

Back To Bridlington

We all knew Mum wasn't going to get better and Dad decided he wanted us all to have one last holiday together in and around Bridlington where we had spent so much of our lives together. We visited all the places we had been to so often as children, and took some photographs to replicate those that had been taken when we were small. One particular photo was at Hutton-Le-Hole, where the village sign was set into a decorative wall. Chris and I stood either side of the sign as we had as children. We revisited all our favourite places, travelled all over the Yorkshire moors and Chris, Dad and I went onto Bridlington beach to write 'Bum' in the sand one last time for Mum to be outraged at.

For me the holiday was a bit odd. It felt unnatural and the big elephant that travelled with us about Mum's impending departure was ever present. I remember walking along the promenade for a little walk and Mum had to keep stopping to get her breath back, but some of the things we did were very nostalgic.

As a child, we rarely stayed in the caravan in the evenings and after tea we would normally go for a walk. One of my favourite places to visit at any time of the day was Sewerby Park. Although it was within walking distance of the caravan, we normally we went in the car and parked in the grounds. Sewerby had the most wonderful formal walled garden, in the middle of which was a fish pond with a fountain. There was also a big conservatory where tender plants and seedlings were raised and the whole effect of the walled garden was hypnotic to me. I remember learning that part of the function of one wall was to absorb the heat of the day and encourage tender plants to grow in an otherwise unsuitable climate. I could imagine in times past, the household being presented with unusual fruits from the walled garden to impress visitors to the hall. The heady scent of old roses in the rose garden beyond the main walled garden, mixed with the geraniums and other plants, is something I can still remember now.

As children, we would run around the flower beds enjoying the noise of the crunch of the gravel underfoot. Mum always had a damp tissue and small plastic bag so that she could pinch a sprig of something from the conservatory area to try and cultivate it at home. With the exception of a lemon scented geranium, invariably it failed, but it never stopped her trying.

Once we had come from the walled garden, we would emerge into the main park area. The path was lined either side with huge monkey puzzle trees which also smelt beautifully of pine and eucalyptus, and at the bottom of the path was a lovely big bandstand. Painted white, we would run up and down the steps as we imagined playing in the band that was there from time to time.

Continuing along we would cross around the outside edge of the croquet lawn and bowling green. Mum would tell us about how she used to pay croquet and we would marvel at the short grass, weed-free bowling green surrounded by crisp white painted ditches where the balls would land out of bounds. Continuing along, we would skirt around the edge of the animal enclosure area. During the daytimes we would sometimes go in and see the animals, but at night we could only see the deer in their large woodland enclosure.

Eventually we would end up at the end of the land mass and arrive at the cliff edge. We would then go left or right and have a walk along the cliffs before returning back to the car.

Soon after I met my husband, I took him there and the smell and feel were exactly the same as I remembered as a child and it made me feel so happy as I could show him first hand somewhere that was so much a part of my childhood and seemed unchanged by the passage of time.

Sewerby Hall is an old house and I found it easy to imagine life in the old days when people lived there and enjoyed the splendour of all it had to offer. At the time when we were children it was rather empty but housed a café, and a small museum dedicated to the life of aviator Amy Johnson. They had her flying suit on a mannequin and a beautiful silk embroidered scarf. It had lots of lovely long fringing and was embroidered in peacock colours. I loved it so much and wished I could have it to wear. The grounds also had a putting green as well as miniature 9 hole golf course. We would occasionally play on the putting green, while Dad watched. He never played with us, it was just us girls and Mum. It was the same with crazy golf. He enjoyed watching us but didn't join in.

We went to all the coves and inlets along the bay of Bridlington, one of which was Dane's Dyke, a local bay with lots of chalk cliffs and chalk beach where we would crack a rock and almost always find a fossil. Heading from there we would drive to Bempton Cliffs, which at the time housed the biggest Puffin colony in Europe. Flamborough Head, North and South Landing were all nearby and regularly we would walk along the coastal path from one to the other. Other outings took us to places like Filey, Whitby, Scarborough, and Spurn Head.

On our last holiday as a family, we visited all these places along with many other wonderful Yorkshire treasures and shared memories of times past before we left it all behind for the last time as a family. We drove along the front for our last look at the sea, which we always did when we left Bridlington, waved goodbye and headed back home. The weather had been kind to us and we were lucky that one memory we didn't replay was the one spending time sitting in the car staring at the steamy windscreen. Dad regularly told us as children, whatever we were doing, we were there to enjoy ourselves and enjoy ourselves we would! It was always done in a jokey sense, but the essence of it has stayed with me all my life. If I'm doing something, I do my best to enjoy it as much as I can.

Happy Days

One of our favourite places to visit was Spurn Point. Also known as Spurn Head, it was a headland created by longshore drift, (remember your geography lessons?) and was quite novel as walking along the lovely beach, we had the North Sea on one side of us and the river Humber on the other side. In recent times, Spurn has been allowed to acquiesce to nature and it seems a lot of the road we used to drive along has washed away. The buildings have long since disappeared but its beauty remains albeit in a different way. As the saying goes, time and tide wait for no man, and it's very evident here.

I feel very lucky that as children we had so much fun when used to love to visit Spurn. Generally deserted, it was also home to an outcrop of old war barracks and had an old lookout tower which was decaying.

When we first used to go there, we used to love running up to the top of the tower and looking out over the estuary and the land on either side. As time went on, the tower became more decayed and the iron step ladder that took us to the top had rungs missing as rust took over. Eventually, it all fell into a very poor state and the door into the tower was boarded over. Dad being Dad, he wasn't to be put off by a bit of wood over the entrance so he would push it aside and we would go up to the top, being careful to make sure the steps were still strong enough to hold us.

The people who had the caravan next door to us on one side were a family from Hull. The Mortimer's. Their children, Barbara and Paul, were great fun and Chris and I had wonderful times when they were at the caravan. We would wander around the caravan site occasionally creeping over the wire fence that separated the site from the posh private school grounds that were adjacent to us. We would imagine we saw all sorts of creepy and spooky things in the thicket and between the trees that formed a screen to the school land, and then half frighten ourselves to death as our imagination carried us away and we thought we were being chased.

The Mortimer's lived in Hull. I remember they lived on the Holderness Road and at the back of their terraced house there was a small back yard that led out into the Fortyfoot. The Fortyfoot, I imagine was the distance between the row of houses that backed onto each other. It formed a wonderful place to play and as there were very few cars in those days, we were rarely interrupted by drivers keen to get through to their back yard.

Something very surprising happened whilst I was writing this chapter about the Mortimer's.

I wrote all about them and this chapter one Sunday afternoon. On my own as my husband played golf, it was another lovely journey down memory lane for me as I slipped back in time and felt I was there again, experiencing all the sounds smells and senses of those happy times.

A few days later my sister phoned me, and was almost in hysterics laughing at something. Laughing so much it took a while for her to gather herself to tell me that she had just been relaying a tale to one of her carers about when we were at the caravan and were with the Mortimer's!

I was flabbergasted. Chris and I haven't really spoken about them for over 40 years, and as we lost touch after we sold the caravan, we have no need to talk about them to anyone else let alone ourselves. I told her what I'd been doing a few days before and we shared a spooky sibling moment of togetherness. I'm very glad we are on a similar wavelength for some things as Chris reminded me of a story I had forgotten.

On one of our forays playing around the caravan site one day, we had a naughty half hour as we realised how the gas bottles worked that supplied every caravan. There was no electricity in those days, just gas and solid fuel. We had maybe watched Dad as he changed the bottle, but whatever it was that gave us the idea, we went all around the caravan site turning the gas off on the bottles under people's caravans. This gave us lots of fun thinking of everyone who would be wondering why there was no gas to light the lamps or fuel the cooker, and it was great until we got caught by someone. It was a man who spotted us, but fortunately, we managed to run off before he could identify us, find out who our parents were and tell them. Even better was that by the time he caught us we had managed to get around almost all of the site!

Even if they weren't at their caravan, we would visit the Mortimer's at their home quite often when we were at our caravan, and I remember they liked very strong Yorkshire tea. The teabags were put outside on a huge heap of other teabags to rot down and then be used as compost. The pile outside the back door never seemed to get any bigger or smaller, but it was something I had never seen. We didn't use tea bags in those days. Mum thought they were very uncivilised and insisted on loose tea in a teapot. In fact, Mum was a bit slow getting to grips with new ideas and it was a long time before we had mugs in the house. We always had tea cups and saucers.

Occasionally, the Mortimer children would be at the caravan just with their mother Doreen and she was very glamourous. Short fashionable skirts, and very 1960's, she was a kind and lovely lady. Their Dad Arthur, was more serious and remained back in Hull working during the week so came to the caravan just at weekends.

One particular time, Mum and Dad, invited Doreen and the children to join us on a trip to Spurn Point. With a Morris Oxford, this was easy. It was a big car in those days, and with Mum and Dad in the front, Doreen and the four of us children piled into the back and squeezed in. This was in the days before seatbelts, or the need for regulation of any kind of passenger numbers. With common sense and a big enough engine, we had a great time as we arrived with a picnic and a sunny day to Spurn Point. We took them up the tower, which by now was almost impossible. Dad had to lift us to reach the bottom of the rapidly disappearing iron ladder, but we all got there and back safely, and we had a few photos taken to prove it.

Back down on terra firma, we children went exploring in the old barracks and surrounding buildings and had a truly wonderful time.

Close to Spurn Point was Withernsea, which was quirky to us as the lighthouse was in the middle of the town. We found it very odd to be there instead of on the edge of a cliff or on rocks in the sea, and a bit further along from there was Hornsea, more particularly Hornsea pottery. In those days, Hornsea was famous for its lovely pottery and we would visit regularly and have a wander around the factory where we could watch the potters at work, and then go into the shop to see the finished items. This was the place Mum eventually succumbed and allowed us to buy some mugs. They were blue shiny glazed and had a brown edge to the top of the rim. There was a pretty pattern of flowers on the side and Chris and I felt very modern with our new mugs.

As a prolific producer of pottery, it's hard to imagine that it all eventually stopped trading. I often see their wares in charity shops and remind me of our times in Hornsea.

Back in Hull, we would walk along the dock-side. This was another favourite activity for me and one of my very favourite family photographs was taken at the docks. Rarely did we have a photo of the four of us together, but this was one that was taken for us by one of the Mortimer's and we are all happy on it.

It's hard to imagine now how we had unrestricted access to the docks. The huge ships were moored by their huge ropes and we could walk over to them and touch them. I was fascinated by the size of the ships and we would walk to where we could watch the ferries leaving and arriving through the harbour.

This, along with seeing the original Titanic film, A Night To Remember, gave me a yearning to go on a ship and I decided when I grew up, I would go on one of these luxury liners, where I could dress up and be treated like a princess. I would buy a trunk from Lewis's in Birmingham and fill it with beautiful clothes for the trip. My imagination was better than the actual reality, but I was too young to know that the ferries weren't cruise liners. They looked huge and appealing. One was called the Norwind, and went to and from Rotterdam.

One day, we were walking along the dockside and the Norwind was creeping out from her mooring through a very narrow channel that led to the sea. All of a sudden, a clamour was heard as a man came racing along the side of the dock shouting at the ship and waving his umbrella furiously, trying to attract attention. The ship's staff saw him and must have told the captain and the ship came to a gentle stop. A rope ladder was dropped down the side of the ship and someone in a small tender appeared. The man climbed down a set of steps on the side of the dock, into the tender and they rowed back over to the ship where he clambered up the rope ladder to board the ship.

Even in those days it was a bit of a surprise that they let him board in such a way, but they did. No-one was hurt and the ship glided off into the big blue sea, with her full passenger cargo.

Fireman's Lift

When Mum was poorly, life changed a lot. As she became very weak, eventually, we needed to get her bed moved downstairs. We would take it in turns to help Dad put her to bed and use the commode but eventually, she was confined to being upstairs and it was decided to bring Mum and her bed downstairs. She was petrified.

We rearranged the lounge, got a single bed and all was set. Dad seemed to think it was just a matter of picking up Mum and carrying her down. Dad was strong and Mum was very slight by this time, but she was also in a lot of pain if she was moved in the wrong way, and absolutely terrified. She burst into tears.

Fortunately, across the road from us lived a fireman and his wife and family. We were good friends and Chris and I played with their daughters and went to each other's birthday parties as we grew up. Dad had a brainwave. In those days, firemen had to be able to carry people out of burning buildings and so he was asked if he would come and carry Mum downstairs. Although she was still very scared and kept her eyes firmly shut, she allowed him to carry her and he very gently scooped her up and brought her safely down.

Life then settled into another pattern. It made life better for Mum as she wasn't confined to the bedroom and she could partake in life a bit more normally. We could also get her up and into her chair. At night, Dad rigged up a phone so that if she needed anything she just needed to dial it and it rung upstairs. Dad would get up and then get either me or Chris to help him. Normally, it was to use the commode, but after she was given some sleeping tablets, we had several days of mayhem as they made her hopelessly confused and she didn't know where she was, what day it was, or what time. She was very distressed and we were too. It was probably the most stressful and upsetting time of the whole of her illness for me. Normal Mum had effectively disappeared and become a nervous, confused other person. I thought it was the end. The night before my second driving test, I was up with Dad eight times. Hardly surprising that I failed!

Luckily and very quickly we realised it was the medication and stopped the tablets. Mum came back to being herself and we all breathed a sigh of relief.

8th December 1980

It was a Monday. It was 6.30pm, and my darling Mum went to sleep for the last time. Three and a half months before my 18th birthday.

It had been a strange sort of weekend prior to this and some peculiar things happened.

On the Friday, for no reason whatsoever, Dad decided to go and fetch a colour chart for the new company car he was going to be having. He hadn't thought about it or discussed it with anyone, he just had a thought that afternoon and got the chart. He knew Mum was ailing and thought it would be nice if she could choose the colour of his car for him.

He also decided to contact the people in charge of decommissioning the power station, opposite the office he worked in, to ask if he could go and have a look around it. The man on the phone said he'd be delighted to take him around and so Dad went over during the Friday lunch time.

As they were walking around, the man started talking to Dad about Mum. He had never met my dad, didn't know him in any capacity, but told him all sorts of things about Mum and Dad, and he said he knew how ill Mum was. But most importantly, he told Dad, 'It's time to let her go.' He said it was only Dad's will that was keeping Mum alive and she needed to go.

Dad came back to the office, and when he went home my Godmother was there. She had been round to see Mum and she felt something wasn't right. Mum seemed to be delirious and had kept on and on about 'telling them the colour of the car.' She couldn't make any sense of it and so decided to stay until someone came home. As soon as Dad went in, Mum told him to 'pick the green one.'

On the same Friday as I was at work, Gerry, my supervisor came to me and bent down next to me at my desk. She asked if I was all right. I said yes, I was fine. She asked me again and said I had been sitting there doing nothing but holding my pen and staring into space for the last half hour. I had no idea. I had clearly drifted off somewhere and all I could remember was thinking about Mum. I started to cry, and apologised for not working. I thought I was in trouble, but she said not to worry, I wasn't in trouble she just wanted to make sure I was all right. In those days, any trauma in the office was dealt with in the ladies toilet, so as was protocol, she then took me into the ladies toilet and mopped my tears.

It was a strange thing. The ladies toilets on the first floor in Parham House, West Bromwich, were very unpleasant. With no natural ventilation, they weren't the nicest place to be, but for whatever reason, in there, people broke their hearts, shared secrets, and all manner of whatever was happening in their life. It was all imparted in those toilets. If you went in and something was going on, you just went about your business and said nothing. It was as though nothing untoward was happening. If you were there on matters of other reasons, you confided with confidence that anyone who came in would ignore you politely.

The day before Mum died was a Sunday. I sat with Mum for a bit and I started to become very upset. I felt as though I couldn't control my tears and not wanting to cry all over Mum, I went to see my Godmother. I had a good weep all over her and she told me she would go and see Mum the following day and spend some time with her. I went to see my boyfriend. His mum, who regularly used to call to see my mum, had crocheted her a beautiful bed jacket, cared for me, fed me and gave me lots of love.

On the Monday, I got home and Mum was very frail and tired. She was eating very little, just beef soup and tinned strawberries. I fed her and as she leaned on me for support, she was so weak and frail, it was awful to see. She was in a lot of pain and so very quickly, we lay her back down and made her comfortable. It all became too much for me and I felt the tears welling up again. I kissed her and went out of the room and started up the stairs to my room, tears were rolling down my cheeks.

I was only half way up and Dad called. 'Mum is going.' I dashed downstairs, Chris ran in too and Dad told us to say goodbye. Chris rushed and got her Christmas present from the two of us, ripped open the paper and wrappings, and sobbingly told Mum we had bought her some perfume. She sprayed it on her and Mum smiled.

Dad kissed her goodbye. Then Chris kissed her and I was last. I wanted to be the last person to kiss her goodbye and as I did, I told her I loved her and she quietly slipped away.

It's as fresh and real to me now as it was when it happened. At the time of writing, that is nearly 42 years ago. It's very rare I feel sad about her leaving us now, she was tired and needed to go, but writing this made me cry. I was right there again, as it all happened.

The next part is rather odd and surreal. After three and a half years of fighting to live, and our lives being turned upside down, it was all over. We all stood around not knowing what to do.

My Dad, being completely Dad, went and got his camera and took some photos of her. Whilst I think this was the most bizarre and utterly inappropriate thing to do, none of us know what we will do in the face of the devastation of grief so I don't condemn him for it, but heaven only knows what the people who developed the photos must have thought. Thankfully, the photos were later destroyed.

We phoned Mrs Fieldhouse and Joan, my Godmother, who both came round immediately. Mrs Fieldhouse brought a mirror to put to Mum's mouth and nose to see if any breath was there and once we were sure she had left us, the doctor and the undertaker were called.

We all felt numb and didn't know quite what to do next. Sometime later we put the TV on and heard the news that John Lennon had just been shot dead. Shocking as it was, I smiled as I felt he and Mum held hands and went happily up to heaven together. She deserved someone special to take her there.

I remember phoning into work the next morning and telling Gerry, Mum had died. She told me to let her know when the funeral was and said I got five days special leave, and that if I wanted any more time off to ask.

We went to arrange the funeral and it was to be a few days later. We ordered flowers and Dad arranged to go and see Mum in the chapel of rest the following day. I instantly didn't want to go.

Next day and Chris, Dad and Nan were all set to go and see Mum. I really didn't want to go but I didn't want an interrogation into why I didn't want to go so I just kept quiet and went. I thought I'd try and keep in the background. No such luck though. We were shown into the room and they all took it in turns to go to Mum and kiss her. I was freaking out inside! I absolutely didn't want to kiss my dead Mum, but again, couldn't face a discussion so obediently followed suit.

It wasn't pleasant. She was icy cold and looked all wrong. It took years to get the image and feeling out of my head and replace it with all the nice ones again.

On the day of the funeral, as was custom in those days, the whole of the street kept the curtains closed. Cars came to the house, all the flowers were arranged on the lawn and then put in the hearse. We drove off and as we turned onto the dual carriageway that led to the crematorium, I turned and looked behind. There were so many cars behind, it made me feel elated. Mum was such wonderful person and so well loved, she had attracted a glorious trail of cars in the wake of the hearse.

As I got out of the car, Gerry handed me a big bouquet of flowers and all of the people on my section from work were standing with her. I felt immensely comforted to see them there.

I hardly cried during the service. It all seemed a bit odd. I was glad that Mum was out of pain and free of her suffering. I had the next few days off work and then went back. Dad said there was nothing to be gained from sitting at home and the sooner we all got back to a normal routine the better. Harsh as that may sound, he was right. There was no counselling in those days, we just had to get on with it all.

It didn't diminish the grief and loss that we were suffering, but it did put some sort of normality back to our lives and distracted us from the heavy loss we all felt.

We were also, all quite exhausted. Emotionally and physically. We had had disturbed nights and lost sleep for a long time and like it or not, we had all been waiting for the day when Mum had to leave us, which in itself was very draining.

A week later we went to church, as was protocol, to Evensong. We all sat in a line and strangely, it was the first, and as far as I can remember the last time I ever heard my Dad actually sing.

Back at work and lots of people came to give me their condolences. I remember particularly Richard, who came to see me. He was, and still is a wonderfully kind man. He knelt down next to me and told me he knew how I must feel as he had lost a family member and he said, 'you will never get over it, but you will get used to it and then it will become easier.' I can see him telling me this as clearly as when he said it. He was wearing a blue checked flannel shirt and grey trousers. He was very tall and it was the first time I had ever seen him from above as he looked up at me. He made me feel so warm and soothed. Years later, he went on to become a missionary and preacher, and went to Albania to help spread the gospel. He still does amazingly wonderful work.

I was very blessed to have had the most wonderful mother and although she had to leave me, the lessons she taught me have, I hope, stayed with me all my life.

'Always look at the other person's point of view before your own,' is a particular favourite.

She taught me to cook, clean, speak properly, have certain standards and morals, never compromise on your integrity, be as honest as you can, and embrace the weaknesses of yourself and others.

Life after Mum

To begin with it was all a bit empty. Our lives weren't revolving around taking it in turns to get up at night, getting home in time to help put Mum to bed and help her using the commode. People were very kind to us and we often had food parcels brought to us to help us on our way.

Eventually, life took on a new sort of normal. Chris and I looked after ourselves, and Dad cooked his own lunch and tea during the week. He invariably had tinned peas and always left at least one pea on his plate which always ended up on the draining board. It used to irritate me so much as I couldn't understand why he couldn't just eat it on the plate, or remove it. I can still see it now, wrinkled and cold, lying around on the draining board. I got to think he didn't like washing up so leaving a pea would mean someone would have to move it and clean down the sink in the process. Whatever the reason was, I often used to leave it there to make a point, and it made me even more mad when he dared to criticise my cleaning. I would remind him that he was the one who left it there!

Mum died just before Christmas in 1980 and so Christmas that year was another strange occasion. No-one wanted to celebrate and it all passed by in a strange blur of misery.

We adjusted to our new life, and to be fair to my Dad, it must have been very difficult as he was grief struck losing his wife, and left with two teenage girls. He had always been the breadwinner whilst Mum stayed at home to take care of us all and our home. We all knew how to clean, cook and keep house, but we didn't have any instructions on how to live without Mum. As I said, I don't think counselling existed in those days so we just got on with things. The weeks passed, they turned into months and then it was a year.

At the same time that Mum had died, on the first anniversary of her death, I was out, but Dad and Chris were at home. They both saw a very strange 'disturbance' pass around the lounge.

On the second anniversary, Chris and I were at home alone and at the time Mum died, all the lights fused spontaneously in the house. We had to get hold of Dad to come and fix it.

We experienced lots of unusual happenings over the years, and often, when we were in the kitchen, Dad and I would both turn as we heard what sounded like Mum whistling through the letterbox. It wasn't a sound like the wind creating a whistle, it was always a proper tune like Mum used to whistle.

I don't want to challenge people's beliefs here, or say whether what we experienced was explainable by other means, but for us, at the time it happened, and the manner with which we experienced it, we all knew it was Mum.

Another Skidmore Christmas

The second Christmas after losing Mum, just over a year since it all happened and Christmas was once again upon us. You probably know by now, Christmases were often a source of misery in our house for one reason or another, and is probably the reason as I've become older, I don't get excited over it. I'm pleased to say my husband more than makes up for it and is ready to go shopping in October, and plan the food we need to buy weeks in advance. I always tell him not to let me dampen his spirit and love for the festive time. I enjoy it at a distance.

Sadly, this second Christmas was another one to remember for all the wrong reasons.

Chris and I used to put up the Christmas tree and decorations, the weekend after Dad got the tree down from the loft, which was sometime in December. This year, he chose to get it down on a Monday evening, and by Friday was grumbling about us not putting it up, and saying if we didn't put it up, he would put it back in the loft.

Chris saw red! She had been putting the cards up around the lounge and dining room, in our time-honoured fashion, over the last few days a bit at a time. Between us, we had lots of Christmas cards and we used to hang them on fancy strings with pegs from the picture rail. We were both working full time and hadn't had time to put the tree up and had been planning to do it at the weekend. Filled with annoyance, Chris told Dad to put the tree back in the loft, and promptly took all the cards down, sorted them into relevant piles and put them on our respective beds. Chris put hers up in her bedroom. Dad and I didn't bother.

Still not learning he needed to try harder, Dad then went into a proper bah-humbug sulk that would have made Scrooge look like the laughing policeman. He decided he didn't want to partake in Christmas and as time grew nearer, he just became more and more grumpy.

Chris entered into the spirit of his grumpiness by digging her heels in. She said if he didn't want to join in with Christmas he could go ahead and sulk. She wasn't going to try and jolly him out of it.

I was cooking the dinner and asked him about what we were going to have. He said he didn't want anything, just a bowl of soup, he said it was just another normal day as far as he was concerned, he didn't approve of the hype and money that was wasted on Christmas. I was mortified. Chris was of the view, if that's what he wants, that's what he can have!

Christmas day arrived. Chris decided that since Dad wasn't going to partake of food and frolics, she would hang the washing out. She had purposely done a big load of washing the night before and had saved it for her party-piece.

In those days, hanging out your washing on a Sunday really was not the done thing, so to do it on Christmas day was an absolute heathen sin. What on earth would the neighbours say? What would God and Jesus think? I was shocked that she would be so bold as to commit such an act of defiance, but also admired her stance.

Dad, said nothing, which was even more surprising.

We came to open our presents and Dad decided he didn't want any. Again, I tried to cajole him into joining in and thought the present we had bought him would be the catalyst for him to cheer up a bit.

Chris had an Olympus Trip camera and had bought an automatic flash to go with it. Dad was constantly borrowing it from her to use on his camera. He used the old-fashioned bulbs that used to fit into a fan-shaped flash and were single use. We decided we would buy him a flash gun like Chris's and it would save him money and effort with the old bulbs. It was quite expensive and we were really pleased to find a gift that was a surprise and also something that we knew he would use. Dad wasn't interested in presents and his general request was for razor blades and Brylcream. Occasional pants, socks and pyjamas completed the list.

So, as we persuaded him to open his gift from us, even Chris was looking hopeful and pleased.

Dad had other ideas! He looked at it, asked why on earth we had bought it and said he had no desire for one. We were flabbergasted, devastated and angry, all in equal measure. He discarded it to one side. He then proceeded to open some other gifts that had been bought for him and literally, tossed them to one side declaring he didn't want it, and what a waste of money they were.

Chris took the gifts away, including the flash gun, and said, 'no problem, we will take it back and get a refund.'

Dad, then left the room and went out in the car.

Chris was in rebellious mood, so decided we were going to continue Christmas with or without our petulant father, so declared we would get Mum's car and go and see all the people we normally did on Christmas morning. We would then collect Nan and return home for Christmas dinner.

For several years, on Christmas day morning, my friend Carolyn came to see me on Christmas day on her pony. As we got older, we used to go to see her and her mum. We would then go to some other friends. Mum and Dad knew them and they had 3 children. They were a very jolly, happy family and always seemed to be laughing. A couple of hours on Christmas day at their house made our day. Always welcoming, Mum and Dad would talk downstairs and Chris and I would be absorbed by the lovely chaos of their present opening, running about enjoying the day. I remember vividly one Christmas Day morning going there and they had the brand new, just released, Michael Jackson video, 'Thriller.'

We felt very privileged to watch this story-with-music, which was unique at the time. Everyone wanted to see it and the hype surrounding its release was huge. Remember this was before internet, multi-channel TV and everything that nowadays gets leaked.

As we got older, we might even have a little tipple of alcohol whilst we were there.

So, taking Mum's car, (Which we never did without asking permission), we went to see Carolyn and her mum, and then up to our family friends. We explained what had happened with Dad and they were all very kind to us and made us feel more 'normal' again.

Next thing was to get to pick up Nan. She lived very close to us and usually walked down to us. We wanted to make sure we got to her before she could bump into Dad, should he reappear.

We caught up with her just as she was leaving her house. She was really pleased we had thought to pick her up, until we told her about Dad. She was just about to head into a weepy sob and Chris told her to stop snivelling. Chris said we weren't going to have Christmas ruined by Dad.

Arriving home, we exchanged presents and I finished preparing the dinner. Once served, we sat down to eat. Just as we were tucking into our roast beef dinner, (we weren't keen on turkey) Dad arrived. We all looked at one another and I asked Chris if I should get him a dinner.

'No! He wanted soup so that's what he can have. He's spoiled our Christmas so he can just have a bowl of soup.'

So reluctantly, that's what I got for him. He sat at the table with us, we continued chatting between ourselves as if nothing had happened, and Dad said nothing.

Afterwards, he disappeared into his shed and life went back to normal.

As much as Dad was so grumpy that day, the thing that upset me more than anything was something else he failed to do.

Every year, without fail, Mum would buy Chris and me a bag of sweets. She put lots of various different chocolate bars and other types of sweets, in a plastic bag, and put it under the tree.

No fancy wrapping, but it was something we both loved and was a real treat. Dad got nothing for us. He gave us money to buy ourselves whatever we wanted to, which was lovely, but I'd really hoped he would have just gone to the effort of getting us our bag of sweets. It's often the small things that hit us the hardest, and whilst Mum was the one who did everything like that, I was really upset and disappointed that Dad hadn't had the thought to get us anything that didn't involve him handing over money.

I appreciate Dad didn't buy into what he saw as the commercial driven behaviour of birthdays, Christmas, Fathers and Mothers Days, but he also failed to see that a small token of thought could make people feel valued, loved and give some pleasure.

We had another episode of this the following year after Mum died, when he refused to get Nan, his mother, a Mother's Day card. I went and got one for him and gave him a pen to write it, but he refused. We ended up having a row in the garage as I told him he was thoughtless and told him how just signing a card would make Nan feel so happy and appreciated, but he absolutely refused. Knowing how upset she would feel, made worse by the fact that it highlighted Mum not being with us, I wrote the card and bought a little glass violet vase for her. She was thrilled I had thought of her and I think it made up for Dad being his usual self.

He would grudgingly get Mum a birthday card, always under duress. One weekend, he was called out to some friends who owned a small Post Office. There had been a fire and they needed him to sort the wiring out. He came back with a handful of smoke damaged birthday cards, which were also faded and jaded and put them in a cupboard. Every year from then, he would take one out to give to Mum. She didn't seem to mind, I suppose she got used to it and accepted it as part of his character, and until we lost Mum, it never really affected the rest of us.

We all got over it and when he met and married my step-mother a few years later, she made sure we all got the cards and presents on time.

Funnily enough, many years later, I remember it being Dad's birthday and when I phoned to wish him happy birthday, he complained that he hadn't had a card from me! He was really upset that it hadn't arrived and waited for the post the following day to phone and tell me happily that his card had appeared, albeit a day late. How things change!

Joan

Joan Oldhams. My Godmother. She was an amazing woman and the wisest person I ever met. I always thought of her as an owl. She was kind, scrupulously fair, but didn't suffer fools gladly. She had a brilliant wit, wonderful sense of humour, and although I never remember her overtly criticising anyone, she had a way of looking that told you she wasn't approving sometimes. If I ever wanted to know anything in truth, I would ask Joan.

She gave me some wonderful words and phrases which I have used all my life. In the face of adversity, she would say,

'It all brings us closer together.'

When things got complicated, she said,

'The older we get, the greyer life becomes.'

If we were wanting to know something that was going on, she said,

'We are just being curious!'

Hence, I was thrilled to find out one day, that Joan and I had the same heroine. Pollyanna.

Pollyanna, in the face of any adversity would always find something to be glad about. I am an optimist and I always look for something positive in every situation, however unrealistic that might be.

After Mum died, Dad and I really didn't get on well at all. I found out later that Mum had asked Joan to mediate and keep her eye on us. She did it brilliantly.

Whenever Dad had upset me, and in my view become completely unreasonable, I would charge round to Joan and tell her all about it. I found out later, Dad often did the same about me!

Joan had the ability to sympathise with me without appearing to take sides, and set it all right. She rarely, openly criticised my Dad, neither did she criticise me, she just made me feel that I wasn't being unreasonable and soothed my raw emotions.

Later on in life, she was more open with what she thought about some of the incidents, and I'm pleased to say, she was invariably on my side, and agreed that Dad had an 'unusual' outlook on things.

On my 18th birthday, Joan offered to have a birthday party for me. It was just a few weeks after Mum had died and things were still very odd at home as we tried to settle into some sort of life without Mum.

It was a lovely evening. The usual crowd of friends came, even Dad came, and he hated parties. Joan had made a cake and a photo was taken of Dad and me cutting the cake. I remember feeling really awkward and said it felt like we were cutting a wedding cake!

When I bought my first car and Dad told me I couldn't park it outside the house, I went to Joan and complained about it. Joan did agree he was being unreasonable, but said to park it up the road from their house and wait for the dust to settle. She said curiosity would get the better of Dad and he would soon come round. She was right. She knew he just didn't like the fact that with my own car, I was independent and he couldn't stop me going wherever I wanted to. It certainly wasn't that he was worried about my safety, he didn't worry about things like that and we rarely had accidents like people do now.

I spent hours and hours at Joan's. Joan, and Derek, her husband, didn't really go to other people's houses, everyone went to them, it always felt like open house and there were often people dropping in. We used to drink tea, and there was always lots of laughter, (in between my traumas).

Liz, Joan's daughter was between Chris and me in age, so in a different year group, but I used to spend a lot of time with Liz in my teenage years as we both used to belong to the school walking club and often went walking together. We had the same circle of friends.

Liz's two cousins were also part of our social circle, they weren't at our school but we saw them regularly and their parents organised lots of events for cancer research. For three consecutive years, we all did a 20 mile sponsored walk for cancer research. Once was from Dartmouth Park in West Bromwich, to Bewdley, another was from Dartmouth Park to Whittington Barracks in Lichfield, and the third time was Whittington Barracks back to Dartmouth Park. The last one was a bit of a problem as we were all bussed over to Lichfield in a double decker bus. Getting to a bridge, we only just cleared the height by a few inches as the bus crept underneath and we all held our breath, not least the bus driver. I've no idea how he got back, as the bus was somewhat weighted down with us all on the way there!

During the walk to Bewdley I remember vividly walking down Hagley Hill past the obelisk. I thought what a wonderful place it would be to live. Little did I know years later, I would move to live a couple of miles away.

Before mum died, she was in the process of knitting me an Aran jumper. Being so poorly it was a really difficult task to complete. I know she wanted to finish it, but she didn't quite make it. I was so sad about it and told Joan. After mum died, Joan finished the jumper for me, and it seems very fitting that the two most important ladies in my life joined together to make it for me. I still have it.

Sometime, also after mum died, Joan gave me a gift of some fabric, 6 hexagons sewn together, and some spare paper hexagons. She suggested I use some of mum's enormous collection of fabric and make a patchwork quilt. She said each piece would remind me of something about our life as mum had used the fabrics to make our clothes, curtains, tea cosies and all manner of other things. She was right. All done by hand, it was easy to begin with but then became so big it was difficult to manage so I put it down for long periods of time. It was a true labour of love and took me 12 years to finish, but I did it. I ended up using other fabrics that I'd used making my own things too and a few bits of fabric I picked up along the way that I liked. I finished it all by hand, and it contains well over 1,000 hexagons. In later life I made several square patchwork quilts for people I knew at work but never hand sewn, always on the sewing machine. I often went home on a Friday and presented it to them on the Monday.

After Mum died, my Godmother was the person I respected and trusted most. She lived to be 92 and I aspire to be like her in old age.

An Empty Space.

Things between Dad and I wobbled along as we regularly clashed over things. Dad didn't like me having a boyfriend and made no secret of the fact that he really wanted Chris and me to be at home looking after him, so made things difficult and awkward. To be fair to him, he was as lost without Mum as Chris and I were. Chris was much less prone to show her emotions than I was, and I know Mum had asked Joan to keep a quiet eye on Chris. Apparently, Mum had said something like,' you won't need to ask Gill, she will let you know, but Chris keeps it all to herself.'

Despite my optimistic nature, there were times when life was thoroughly unhappy for me.

I had lots of friends, and during the times I felt unhappy at home, I would do my best to keep away. I regularly went to friend's houses and when I had a boyfriend, I also went there. I had my car and that was somewhere I felt safe and at ease. At one particular time, I was really upset with life and Dad in particular, so I would leave for work in the morning by 7.30 and not return until I knew he had been back home and gone out again. I would eat my tea and go out again not returning until well after I believed he was in bed. The longest period I managed to avoid seeing him properly was 4 weeks. It's hard to imagine living in the same house as someone without seeing them for so long but I managed it. Sometimes, I would go home and see the lights on in the lounge. Chris went out with her boyfriend to the pub every night and then straight to bed so I knew it was Dad who was still up. Maybe he was waiting to see me, I never knew, but rather than face a confrontation with him, I would just drive off and come back later when the house was in darkness.

One particularly miserable time, Dad was trying to impose some sort of restrictions upon me and he was being really unpleasant. Again, I can't really remember the trigger for it, but he told me that if I didn't want to live by his rules, I could go and find myself somewhere else to live and see how I got on. If it didn't work out, I could then come back home and live by his rules.

I cannot begin to explain how menacing, threatening, cold and uncaring this made me feel. Dad clearly saw things differently to me in many things and he struggled to deal with having sole responsibility for two teenage daughters, but that didn't help the way I felt. These days, leaving home as a single girl isn't unusual, but in my day, in our world, unless you were abandoned, the only way to leave home was to be married.

189

Often at these times, I would drive up to the Expressway at West Bromwich and drive from one end to the other going around the islands up and down to pass the time. I listened to the radio and sometimes would feel so miserable I would have tears streaming down my face. I remember sometimes wondering about just driving into the railings that surrounded the motorway island and ending my misery, but strangely one thing that made me not keen to do it was fearing that if I didn't kill myself, Dad would go mad at me for deliberately crashing my car! It never, ever crossed my mind that he would be upset or mortified that I was so unhappy with him and my life I wanted to end it all. This thought only crossed my mind a few years ago and I'm glad he never knew. I'm sure he would have been devastated.

Acne & Antibiotics

I can't remember exactly how old we were, but when Chris was around 14, she started to suffer with what we called teenage spots. I'm not sure if they bothered her or not, but she was taken to the doctor and came back with two things. Antibiotics and a skin cleansing scrub. The antibiotics were oxytetracycline which she took twice a day, and the scrub was called 'Brasivol Number 1.' It was a thick paste and contained bits of aluminium oxide grains which was designed to scrub off the dead skin and excess oil. It was very good to use and had a particular pleasing smell which I still remember. Around two years later, and I started getting a couple of spots and was immediately taken to the doctor and given the same. That's just how it was. We both took our tablets and scrubbed our faces and had it all on repeat prescription.

One day, Chris decided she was going to stop taking the antibiotics. She said she didn't think they were working and so I did the same. We had enough Brasivol to scrub most of West Bromwich, so continued to use that for a long time, but we noticed no difference not taking the tablets.

Chris worked in West Bromwich County Court. It was 50 yards away from where I worked and sometimes, we would meet each other at lunch times and walk into West Bromwich town centre. I used to wear high heeled stiletto court shoes and could walk in them all day without pain or discomfort. I could even run in them without any problems. Chris was opposite. She couldn't keep them on her feet. Anything that hadn't got a strap or wasn't closed in, Chris couldn't walk in. She had a particular way of walking where she seemed to flick her heels up, so shoes were always a problem for her, and possibly made worse by the fact that being small she only took a size 3. One day I had been into the town centre and was walking back in my heels and pencil skirt and saw Chris ahead of me with someone else. They had just crossed the road at the traffic lights and I started to run to catch up with them. Calling out, I got to the lights which had all come to a stop and as I sprinted across the road, my heel caught and I went flying. All the traffic was at a standstill and I felt a complete fool as I fell flat. Recovering as quickly as I could, I jumped up, put my shoes back on and chased after Chris. As I caught up, I suddenly realised it wasn't Chris! I felt doubly stupid having fallen flat and then mistaken someone who wasn't my sister! It was just one of those days. My tights were ruined, my knee was grazed, but my pride was dented most of all.

Chris mentioned that when she walked into the town, by the time she got back to work her legs were tingling and asked if mine ever felt like that.

They didn't. Sometime later I asked her about it again and she said it was still happening, in fact it was worse, but it didn't seem to trouble her in any other way so she ignored it.

One Saturday morning, Chris woke up and I went into her bedroom. She told me she couldn't see out of one eye. I was confused and asked her what she meant. She said she was blind in one eye and could see nothing. She didn't seem overly scared by it, but I was shocked. She didn't do anything about it there and then, but went to the optician and they diagnosed optical neuropathy. As I mentioned, this can be a precursor to MS, and I think Chris knew about it. We didn't have the internet then but she worked with a lady who suffered with MS so maybe had learned about it from her. After 2 weeks, her sight returned in that eye, but then she lost her sight in her other eye. Only after Dad dropped something on her head did it all return to normal.

Some years later she started suffering other symptoms but it was only when she developed what looked like Bell's palsy, where one side of her face dropped, that they tested her for MS. She had a lumbar puncture and it was confirmed. Chris had Multiple Sclerosis. She seemed to take it all quietly. No hysteria or why me, and clearly by the time it was diagnosed, she already knew in her own mind what it was.

Thankfully Mum hadn't been alive when it happened. She had died with both her girls being fit and healthy. As you can imagine, Dad was devastated.

He wasn't very good at dealing with things that he couldn't fix, like lots of people and (in my slightly controversial sexist opinion), especially men, and of course being his child, it was a terrible shock. Dad had no idea about MS and his main default mode was to develop a slightly spaniel looking expression and keep asking Chris how she was. Chris understandably got really cross with him and pretty much refused to discuss it. He couldn't pay for it to go away, he couldn't make it better and there was no cure. He could do nothing.

Chris was 27 when she received her diagnosis, but had been having symptoms for years. The tingling in her legs was a symptom and had been happening since she was around 21.

The good news was she had MS in the form of relapsing-remitting, so that meant she had lots of times where, apart from her tingly legs, and her eyesight getting slowly worse, she was pretty much symptom-free. Chris lived her life to the full and said she wanted to do as much as she could so that if the disease took hold, she would have plenty of happy memories to think about. She went all over the world with her partner, John. They joined the National

Trust, went on the Orient Express, ate lovely food and generally did all the things they wanted to do while Chris was able. Chris has never been extravagant, quite the opposite, she was recycling before the word was invented!

MS is a neurological condition where the person's immune system gets out of control and starts attacking the brain nerves that send the messages of sense, and movement. It creates scarring and impedes messages getting from the brain to various areas of the body, and muscles don't function properly. Everyone is different in the way they are affected. There is no cure, the medical treatment is advancing but not until they find the cause will they really get to grips with it. Conversely though, people with MS rarely get ill, since their immune system is on such high alert, it kills everything. Once Chris had MS, she didn't suffer colds, flu, sore throats or the general ailments the rest of us do.

I was the opposite. I was very prone to throat infections. I would feel absolutely fine, then out of nowhere, the roof of my mouth would itch so much, I wouldn't know how to stop it. I used to rub my tongue across it to try and relieve it, but it didn't make any difference. Within 20 minutes of the itching, I would start to feel ill. My throat would hurt, my skin became so sore I could hardly bear to touch it, even the hairs on my skin were tender. I would start with a temperature and feel dreadful. If I was at work, I'd go home at the end of the day, wrap myself in a blanket to keep warm and after a few days I'd be better again. In between I would feel dreadful and unbelievably tired. I didn't have time off work, I just muddled through and felt things could be much worse. Having had proper flu a couple of times as a child, I felt this was just be being prone to colds and having had the long-term problems with winter coughs after whooping cough, I believed I was just more prone to picking things up. Work came before everything and I rarely had time off sick.

Even into my late 30's I still had occasional episodes where I would get an itchy mouth and drop from being really well to feeling dreadful in 20 minutes. Thankfully as I've got older, it seems to have gone away.

What I now believe, is that both Chris and I had unfortunately suffered from very damaged immune systems from taking the antibiotics for so long. I believed it to be this for many years, and although I had no other evidence to support it, we all now know the problems caused by long term overuse of antibiotics. It was just one of those things. In the same way as I believe the whooping cough vaccine probably saved my life when I was young, I believe the doctor was acting in our best interests at the time, and I am absolutely not comparing my illnesses to that of my sister. I just believe the antibiotics were implicated for both of us in very different ways.

Many years later, Chris and I went to York together for a girly few days. Chris was struggling more with her walking and had a wheelchair. We had a wonderful time together and visited some of the places we had been to as children. It's another reason I love York so much. We went to an Italian restaurant one evening. The staff were lovely, their disabled toilets were fantastic, and while we were eating a middle-aged couple came to sit next to us. After a time, the lady said, 'Can I ask you something?' We said yes, and she said to Chris, 'do you suffer with MS?' Chris said she did and we then got into a lengthy chat about it all.

I told her about my theory of the antibiotics and also told her about how I used to suffer with my problems. Her husband then started joining in and asked if I used to get sore skin, talked about the hair on his body being painful, the way keeping warm was so difficult, pretty much all the symptoms I used to have. He was the first person I'd ever met who understood. He said he had had the same and had been diagnosed with ME and chronic fatigue syndrome some years before.

Chris looked at me and said, 'that's what you used to have!'

I said, 'I know!'

She said, I didn't realise it was that bad, you really were ill then!'

I said 'I know, but to be honest, I don't think I realised at the time either. I just knew I felt awful.'

The lady of the couple sitting next to us looked at her husband and said, 'Oh my goodness, I didn't know it was that bad either!' He had experienced the same as I had and she had just thought he was being a typical man, making it worse than it actually was.

I was so pleased to have met him and finally realised how bad it had been was real. It is of course all a matter of 'thy self.' We cannot experience anyone else's feelings, pain, emotion, heartache and happiness. But it's the closest I've ever been to someone saying 'I know how you felt' and I believed he did.

I am very pleased that the diagnosis of ME/CFS didn't exist when I was young as I'm sure I would have been one of the first in the queue. My management of it was to sleep as much as possible when I felt the need, and was one of the best ways of getting better. I have always believed in sleep being a huge cure for the body. Whilst you are asleep your body can deal with the maintenance and repair work without doing unnecessary tasks. It's certainly worked for me.

Chris also had more predisposing factors to developing MS which are now believed to be implicated. Whilst the antibiotics would have affected her immune system, MS has also been linked to viruses attacking the body and making the immune system overreact. She also suffered prickly heat in the summer, so avoided the sun and always kept in the shade as her skin type was more like Dad's. Vitamin D deficiency is also linked to MS with Scotland having the highest incidence of MS in the world. The shock and trauma to her system of losing Mum was also a likely factor. Trauma has also been linked to the onset of MS. Chris hit the jackpot with it all. It doesn't change anything about her condition. It's one of those things. We were brought up to be quite pragmatic, something I'm glad about.

Only after Chris got to 40 did she get more problems, and eventually she was diagnosed with secondary-progressive MS. It's a term to describe when MS doesn't go into remission, although I believe she is very stable as I write. She has fantastic carers, to whom I am forever grateful, and her partner John has been with her through it all.

Chris's condition is also something that can lead to lots of humour. One thing that happens is her emotions can become cross-wired. It means she can express the complete opposite of what you would expect. One example is that of someone she knows, (thankfully rather well), who one day told her he had some bad news. Chris asked what it was and he told her of someone being diagnosed with bowel cancer. Chris burst out laughing. The more she realised it was the wrong reaction, the more she laughed. The man told her it wasn't funny, and she said she knew that, but laughed all the more. Eventually he started laughing too and then her carer joined in.

If Chris finds something funny, she gets uncontrollable! She gets to a point where she can't breathe, so we have to make sure any hilarity is carefully managed. Once she gets the giggles she can't stop and can easily draw a crowd!

I am also very grateful that it doesn't happen the opposite way where she could become uncontrollably distressed. Only on very rare occasions has Chris had a crushing emotional meltdown. On one such occasion, my husband Graham and I went over to her and tried every which way to cheer her up. She couldn't stop crying and it was so distressing and heart-breaking to see.

We took her out to the park and got some fresh air, and I said I wished I could take her pain away. She thanked me for caring for her and said she would do the same for me if it was the other way around. Graham, looked at her and said, Chris, that's rubbish! You would be terrible at caring for Gilly.

We all looked at one another and burst out laughing. It was so true. It broke the sadness and we all felt much better again.

One reason I am so pleased that Chris has carers is that it is extraordinarily difficult to be a carer as well as a relative. Be it partner, sister, parent, child, friend or relative, you lose the relationship as it becomes entwined with the care. It can destroy the proper relationship as the emotional and physical strain that comes about can be overwhelming. It also means Chris gets proper care, people to interact with that she can share her thoughts and feelings with, and I get to remain as her sister.

From time to time as her care package was reassessed, I would become involved. On one occasion, social services had been to see her and had reassessed her needs. They had reduced the amount of the care package significantly and Chris was understandably very upset about it all, wondering how she was going to manage with less time from her carers.

I took charge and phoned social services. I know they do their best and have limited funds, but it's my sister so all of that goes out of the window!

After a few redirections of my call, I eventually got to speak to the person who had reassessed her package. I was on the list of authorised people to talk so once we got through that I told her the reason I have called is to thank her.

'I'm absolutely thrilled about the new reduced care package for my sister and I wanted to phone and thank you personally for the reassessment.

Clearly surprised, she stuttered to thank me for thanking her. I continued, 'No, really, it's me who is thanking you. I am absolutely delighted to learn than you have reduced my sisters care package.'

I can tell she is slightly off balance and not quite sure what to say.

I tell her, 'I think you all do a fantastic job, I believe you are all highly trained in what you do and carry out your assessments taking everything into consideration before determining the package for any individual, and for that you deserve to be given personal thanks.'

Slightly more relaxed, she agreed it's a difficult job, and that they all do their best to do it all fairly and within the rules.

As we are about to close the conversation, I say to her…

'Just before I go, can I ask you one thing please?'

'Yes,' she says.

'Well, I know I'm not a social worker, and I haven't got your training and other skills, so forgive me for not understanding, but can you just explain to me how my sister's health has improved please?'

'What do you mean?' She asks.

'Well, my sister has MS, I believed it was a degenerative neurological condition and that means she doesn't get any better. Clearly, your decision to reduce her care package needs means her health must have improved and she is getting better. My problem is that I can't identify how or in what way Chris has improved, so can you explain it to me. Don't get me wrong, I am thrilled to know she is improving, but I don't understand in what way, so can you tell me?'

It all went very quiet on the phone.

After a bit of a splutter, she came back and told me it was all to do with funding and they had a finite pot of money and had to share it out. I told her I completely understood that, but that didn't explain which of my sister's current needs had improved enough to have funding for them withdrawn. After a bit more of a chat, Chris's funding was reinstated and actually increased, since it appeared that in fact, she had more needs than her last assessment.

Chris has tried all manner of things to try and help and improve her condition. I absolutely believe that when the cause is identified the cure will be very swift. I think it will be something quite simple but clever. I wouldn't be at all surprised to find the answer will come from the depths of the ocean. In my current working world, the discoveries of how the gut bacteria are implicated in good and bad health is unfolding at a massive rate. We have 90% more bacteria in our gut than calls in our body, which tells me they are important.

Whatever it all is, my sister is amazing, I know the colour of her eyes, and often what she is thinking. She has some very fabulous, individual qualities, and has fantastic carers who I love and appreciate enormously. Chris also has lots of friends who care for her deeply.

She also has John, who has been by her side throughout, and gives me comfort for being there. He is a straightforward, amazingly funny, intelligent and clever man. He soothes my mind as he answers all my world problems and questions when I go over, and also makes great coffee!

As her sister, Chris is unique to me, I love and admire her beyond measure, and of course any trouble we got into as children was because she started it! I'll leave it there!

Time To Move On.

Inevitably, time moves on and we all find our own way to deal with things. Life wasn't brilliant by any means, but we hadn't any choice but to continue. Dad wasn't very good on his own. He enjoyed travelling and visiting places and people, but without Mum, he felt lonely, and the car was empty without her sitting in the passenger seat. I had a big teddy bear that sat on my bed. He was soft and furry and huge. One day Dad asked me if he could borrow him. I said yes, but was curious to know why he wanted him. It was not long before I found out. He wanted to put him in the front passenger seat to fill the empty gap that Mum had left, so that when he was driving, he had something in his peripheral vision to stop him feeling so lonely. I found it very sad and touching and felt really sorry for him. (We weren't always arguing!) On the other hand, humour never being far from my mind, it must have given lots of road users a strange image of a middle-aged man travelling along the highways and byways of England with a big fluffy teddy bear in the passenger seat! Eventually, the grief and stress inevitably became too much and everything went into a meltdown.

It all began when Dad started seeing a new lady friend. She lived in the next street to us and we knew her and her two children who were similar ages to Chris and me.

It was a little time before we knew Dad was seeing her and I was pleased as it took the pressure off being at home with Dad, but Chris wasn't impressed. After a time, Dad would come home and tell us the lady he was seeing, did this and that, 'just like Mum did' and we soon realised that it was not going to end well, as Dad sought a replacement for Mum as a part of his grief. Unfortunately, we weren't wrong.

One evening at tea-time, Chris and I were upstairs and noticed a police car pull up across the road from the house. We automatically knew it was something to do with Dad, who was downstairs. We stayed out of the way as two police officers came to the door. We crept out onto the landing to see if we could hear what was being said, but there was no need as in no time at all we were asked to come downstairs.

Dad was in the lounge with the policeman and the police lady, who mustn't have been much older than her early 20's, took Chris and myself into the dining room.

She told us that they had had a call from the lady Dad had been seeing, and she told them he had called her and told her he had over 200 Distalgesic tablets in the house and was going to take them all. She was at work and unable to do anything, she had called the police. Left over from when Mum died, Distalgesic was a very powerful painkiller and taking more than the prescribed dose, even by a small amount could kill.

I don't remember if we realised until then that Dad had stopped seeing her, but clearly there had been some sort of breakdown in their relationship and had resulted in the day's events.

Chris took hold of my hand and said to me, 'don't you dare cry.'

Turning to the police lady, she said, 'If our father wants to be so selfish, that he wants to take all those tablets and kill himself, and leave his two daughters on their own, let him do it. Just ask him to do it somewhere else so that we don't have to find him!'

I was stunned, but not surprised. I remember looking up and staring at the light fitting in the centre of the room with its green glass and brass coloured shade and blinking to stop myself from crying.

I think the police lady was stunned too. She clearly didn't know what to say or do, but was very kind and gentle. She asked us if we knew where the tablets were and Chris said no, but that in any case, we wouldn't hand them over. If Dad was determined to take them, it was his choice. The police recommended Dad should go to see the doctor for help.

I don't really remember what happened next, but I think Dad had promised them in some convincing way that he wasn't going to take the tablets and had only told her that to frighten and upset her, so eventually they left. Dad sat looking like his world had collapsed and Chris determined to carry on as normal, but was very angry. I can't remember if it was the next day, but sometime later Dad went to see the doctor and came home with a big bottle of pills. They were Valium.

Dad was very sensitive to medication, but feeling as bad as he did, he started to take the tablets. He was told he could take between one and three a day, but clearly with no other instructions, he had no idea of the side effects. I'm not aware that he was offered counselling, I don't think it existed in the way it is these days, so we were all left to flounder through the consequences.

Dad started off with 3 tablets and after a couple of days, it was clear he was in another world of his own. A sort of floaty-air surrounded him and he was completely ga-ga.

He started to get into his car each day after tea, and drive round and round the block, which happened to be also driving past the house of the lady he had been seeing.

Realising we needed to do something, I told him he was taking too many tablets and instead of the 3 a day, he should take one. I made him hand them over and gave him one a day. He became much more lucid over the following days and although Chris was still cross with him, I felt sorry for him and tried to care for him.

In the evenings he just seemed to sit looking forlorn and with no interest in doing anything. Eventually, things started to improve, Dad was more like himself and even though he was still a little spaced-out, he continued to drive as he hadn't been told not to. The edges of his distress were a lot softer and he decided he would go and visit some friends.

Still taking my teddy bear as a willing passenger, he went off one day and when he came back, said he had had a lovely time. He said he had been driving down the motorway at over 70 miles an hour and had his foot to the floor on the accelerator and kept thinking, if he was in the aeroplane on the runway, he could be taking off by now. It was time to take him off the tablets before he killed himself or someone else.

He slowly came back into the real world and seemed much better. But it wasn't to last. Whatever his displeasure with the lady was, he was feeling vengeful. We only found out as odd things began to happen at home.

We had small stones thrown at the windows, plants uprooted and general mischief, but then one evening when Dad was out, Chris and I heard a loud bang. We went to investigate and found a big stone had been hurled through one of the garage windows and landed on the boot of Mum's car. We were shocked and couldn't understand what had happened or why.

Dad came back and we told him what had happened expecting him to go mad, but instead, he just said, 'oh well, never mind, it's probably just kids messing about' and said he would fix it. He replaced the glass and put a thick blanket on the boot of the car in case it happened again.

Chris and I were astounded at his lack of interest and anger, but Chris suspected it was one of the children of the lady Dad had been seeing and eventually we found out it was. We also found out why.

She had started to see another man and Dad was clearly not happy about it so started to misbehave. We discovered he had put superglue in her garage lock, and then put a screwdriver through the wall of the man's tyre. Heaven knows what else he did that we didn't find out about, but needless to say, what was happening to us was a response to Dad's behaviour.

Ably assisted by my Godmother and her husband, we got Dad to realise it had to stop and he must behave himself, which he seemed to do. I'm sure it was all a response to the grief and trauma of losing Mum, but didn't make his actions any the more acceptable. He later told us he had lent her some money and wanted it back, which was much more of an explanation as to his out of character behaviour.

Thankfully, things started to settle down and for a time, peace reigned as we all went about our own lives. Dad would sometimes wait up for me when I was out and we would have some nice chats together before going up to bed. Chris was a different type of personality to me so didn't really engage with Dad over his feelings about things like that. I felt sorry for him and he was at a complete loss without Mum.

Happy Days Are Here Again

Eventually Dad met another lady. It was a few years on from the disastrous relationship he had before, his grief had subsided and he was ready to move on with someone who was not seen as a replacement for Mum.

Her name was Heather and she was a primary school teacher. Sometime after Dad met her, he took early retirement from the MEB and left with a good pension. They married in 1984 and Chris and I were bridesmaids. It was a happy day for me as I wanted Dad to be happy and he needed a companion in life. He wasn't very good on his own and together they did all sorts of things. They both loved travelling and for the first time, Dad was able to go abroad and experience the delights of Europe with Heather. Mum never wanted to travel abroad, she was more than happy in the UK.

Once married, and both free of any responsibilities, they decided to move house. Dad wanted to move, but there was always something holding him back. They looked at all sorts of houses, in all sorts of areas, but there was always some problem with them and time dragged on. They had sold Heather's house that she had shared with her mum until she died, and Heather had moved in with Dad and Chris. I had already moved out, Chris moved later.

Our family home sold quickly and after all the ups and downs of our family life, it was another time to say goodbye.

We all got together for one final time the night before it was handed over, and had fish and chips on the floor in the dining room. All the furniture had gone and it felt very strange. It was a lovely day and after we had eaten, we went out into the garden for one last time and took some photos next to the blackboard with a message of 'Our Last Day At Home. October 1985' Dad had found our old straw sun hats and my old riding hat as he cleared things out and we wore them for the photos. With sentiment in our hearts, we shut the door for the last time and went our separate ways.

For a time after selling the family home, Dad and Heather moved to stay with Nan, who was about a mile away. In true Dad style, he didn't want to pay for a removal van, so bit by bit, things were moved in, on, or behind his car. I remember him strapping a mattress onto the top of his car and it nearly took off! Every time the car moved, the mattress folded in half and driving was impossible. He stopped and tried adjusting it, and in the end, they succeeded by driving with the windows open and holding the mattress down! Next was the metal garden roller. Dad knew it was too heavy to go in the car, and didn't have a tow bar, so strapped it to the back of the car bumper and drove up to Nan's carefully dragging the roller behind him! Thankfully no-one saw him so our embarrassment was saved.

Eventually they found a house in Lichfield. It was a four bedroomed, double garaged, new build and also the showhouse. Dad couldn't seem to find anything wrong with it so they bought it. For the first time, Dad had a house that needed no maintenance. It also had a large garden. Dad got fed up pushing the mower so decided they needed a powered one.

Dad didn't like buying things if he could make something from all the bits and pieces he had accumulated over time, so he had a bright idea and attached a rather large motor to the top of his mower and a long cable. Proudly switching it on, it took off with him across the lawn. Unfortunately, he hadn't put any brakes on it, and it was so powerful he couldn't stop it, so they both ended up in the hedge. A good idea but needed a bit more work!

The house was on a main road and at the time they moved in there wasn't too much traffic. It was double glazed and insulated to the top modern standards, so it was really warm and cosy, but still not enough soundproofing for Dad's ears and after a time, he became more and more annoyed at the sound of traffic hurtling past. It was made worse because cars found it easy to speed along just there. Dad got really cross so would regularly go outside with his video camera wearing dark clothes and point it at oncoming traffic. It worked quite well and certainly made motorists feel unnerved enough to believe that he was a traffic camera operator. He complained to the council and police and nowadays there are speed humps along there.

Soon after they moved in, the stereo came to the end of its life and he spent another few weeks trying out every hi-fi unit on the shelf in Curry's before settling on another one that didn't hiss, whistle or make any other sort of background humming noise that offended his sensitive ears. Fortunately, in those days, Curry's were very understanding and allowed him to try them all out willingly. No need to turn it up to full volume and check with the neighbours this time, since the house was detached.

Having lived through the second world war, understandably one of the places Dad was fascinated by was Germany. As soon as possible after the Berlin Wall came down, Dad and Heather went to visit check-point Charlie where they took bits of the wall and wire before it became a tourist attraction and upon their return, they started to go to evening classes to learn German.

This was a surprise given Dad's dyslexic tendencies, but Heather patiently put post-it notes on household items all over the house and he did quite well at learning lots of them.

Lichfield was twinned with somewhere in Germany and Dad and Heather volunteered to take in some German visitors giving them a taste of English hospitality and experience what it was like living in an English home.

Heather was a great cook, especially when it came to entertaining and decided to make some special dishes for the two elderly ladies who came to stay. Serving the starter, it was a bowl of soup, but unfortunately for Dad it was a gazpacho, made from chilled, raw, blended vegetables. Even more unfortunate was that Heather didn't tell him in advance, and Dad being Dad, he expected a bowl of soup to be hot. Dipping his spoon into his soup and putting it into his mouth he was so shocked that it wasn't what he expected he spat it out. Saying nothing, he then leant over to one of the ladies and put his spoon into her soup and tried hers. That being cold too, he spat that out too! Maybe they thought this was some sort of strange English custom but were soon educated as Dad announced in shocked tones, 'Heather, this soup is cold!' Heather explained it was supposed to be, but Dad wasn't impressed and went to put his in the microwave. The two ladies said nothing and sipped their soup politely.

Dad loved engineering, and watching the rebirth of the steam trains as they were renovated and put back onto the various tracks gave him lots of pleasure. He wasn't interested in travelling on them, he just enjoyed watching them and filming them as they built up steam and chuffed their way along. One of their Lichfield neighbours was also a steam enthusiast and lent Dad one of his precious videos. He was a very particular man, think Martin of 'Ever Decreasing Circles,' very ordered and it was a rare thing for him to lend anything to anyone. Dad found him fascinating and funny. Unfortunately, he hadn't pushed out the tabs on the video and Dad inadvertently recorded something over the top of it. Taking it back to him, Dad gave an unreserved apology and confidently told him that there had been an electrical power surge which had wiped his tape and said it was such a rare occurrence he should keep it as a curiosity. Amazingly, he believed him!

Heather, brought a new life to my Dad and was an impartial friend to me during the often-troubled times I had with him. They lived very happily together for 12 years until Dad died suddenly on 25th March 1996, two days after my 33rd birthday. He was 66.

Time To Say Goodbye

It was a strange weekend. My birthday was on a Saturday and Dad phoned to wish me happy birthday and I thanked him for the cheque he had sent me.

I had had a conversation with him some time before about dying and passing into the spirit world and he had asked me, did I believe in God and how did I know we went to heaven. He was talking to me about death and he was worried that if he died, how he would deal with Mum in the spirit world as he now had two wives. I was really surprised and sad for him that he had been mulling over the question for so long and felt troubled by his divided loyalty.

On the phone he was talking about it again.

I told him that in heaven things didn't work like that and that jealousy didn't exist. Everyone was at peace.

He asked me 'How do you know?

I said, 'Well it's faith isn't it.'

He said 'Is it?'

I was surprised that he was having doubts about the faith that we had always known and although we didn't see a lot of things the same way, one thing I do believe about my relationship with Dad was that whenever he wanted to know something and wanted the truth, he would ask me. He seemed to want to know absolutely that when he died, Mum wouldn't be cross with him for remarrying.

The evening after my birthday, Dad had a heart attack. He was rushed to hospital and died in the early hours. His last words to Heather were 'I do feel poorly' and then he died.

I don't believe he suffered any real pain or distress. He knew he had had a heart attack and had had a 'small' one in the past. From then he was diagnosed with angina and took medication. Dad was a funny soul and didn't like change. He refused to change his doctor from West Bromwich so used my sister's address in West Bromwich. He may have benefitted from a by-pass operation, but we will never know. He would never have been a happy old man if he couldn't have been busy, tinkering about and able to walk. For this, I am glad to know he died quickly whilst he was still able to do all the things he enjoyed.

After Dad died, Heather remained a good friend and step-mother. She stayed fit and active and lived a full and wonderful life, whilst still being interested and caring towards Chris and myself. We had many shopping trips together and Graham and I went on holiday with her and sometimes enjoyed her wonderful cooking skills, especially her flapjack, which was the best I have ever tasted. She lived life at a pace, seemingly wanting to cram in as much as possible. I had a saying to describe her.

'Heather is always on the way to somewhere else before she arrives!' because she always walked through the door announcing,

'I can't stop, I'm on my way to… (somewhere)'

She collected speeding fines that kept her licence busy and went on more speed awareness courses than you can count. Always commenting, 'I couldn't possibly have been going that fast!' Another of her protestations was 'well, when I learned to drive you drove to the conditions of the road, not speed limits!'

Patience wasn't her strong point as it involved wasting time, and she was far too busy to be wasting time, even worse someone else might waste it for her! She also hated housework, which was also a waste of time for her.

Heather died in November 2019 after 2½ years suffering with cancer. We spent a lot of time together again taking her to appointments, helping with care as needed and all manner of things that she needed help with. She remained fiercely independent throughout her illness, and it was only at the very end when she realised she wasn't going to be able to get out of her bed, that she finally let go.

I often said, even though I knew her for around 35 years, I didn't feel I knew her any better when she died to the day I met her. She listened, was quite strongly opinionated, but I never felt I really knew what she felt inside or what went on in her head. When I said this to her friends, they all knew what I meant.

Hey, Lawee!

I started school at Easter just after my 5th Birthday. My classmates and I grew up together as we spent so much time in the same classroom and most of us were still together when we left at around the age of 16.

One of my great delights of modern technology is the wonder that is Facebook. Love it or hate it, (It's all about how you use it in my view) for me it allowed me to rediscover my old school friends.

in 2016, I saw a name appear on Facebook. It was the same as a girl in my registration group at Menzies. I sent her a private message and asked her if she was the same girl I was at school with. Amazingly she was, and asked me if I wanted to join the private Menzies Facebook Group for our school year. I immediately said yes, and within a few minutes I was suddenly reacquainted with so many of my old friends I was completely overwhelmed.

I spent a few hours going through the trail of conversations and felt so at home with these people I had grown up with, it felt, and still does, that I had found a big part of my life that was missing. Within a few weeks, there was a reunion taking place and I couldn't wait to go. I introduced another couple of friends that I was in touch with and whipped up a few people who weren't sure about going such was my enthusiasm to see everyone in person.

I wasn't disappointed. It was like we had only seen each other yesterday!

I was really thrilled to see David Harris there and was amazed that he couldn't remember any of the mischief he had bestowed upon me during our school years. I also discovered that none of my school friends knew my mum had suffered cancer during the last few years we were at school. There was also one person who remembered me very well.

Mark Law. Or 'Lawee' (pronounced 'Loree,') as he was known at school. We had a good old chat and towards the end of the evening, he said, 'Do you remember when you shouted across the 'playground' at Menzies to me when we were about 14/15?

'Er…no. What did I say?'

'Well, you were standing under the staff room, (which was on stilts,) with some other girls and clearly you had just learned something about boys' he said with a glint and wry smile.

I was feeling a bit hot and bothered about what I could possibly have said and asked, 'what on earth did I say?'

'Can you really not remember?'

'No! tell me.'

'You shouted, "Hey Lawee, did you have a wet dream last night?"'

I felt so embarrassed. It all came flooding back! 'Oh my goodness! Now you have said that, I remember! I can remember being under the canopy and shouting across. Oh no...I'm so sorry!'

'No problem, I could have killed you at the time, I was so embarrassed I just grunted something and walked off. It's funny looking back.'

Reminiscing with my old friends makes everything so much more real, no need to set the scene, as they were all there. Talking to Mark, we both said we were very 'asexual.' We didn't think of our friends as boys or girls, except on odd occasions like Mark experienced, we were just people. It was generally a wonderful time of life, even then, not just with the rosy tint of age.

Catching up with each other we started to meet more often and the reunion became a get together as we interact on Facebook, meet for drinks and parties and our respective partners now join us. We all care about one another in a very genuine lovely way and whilst we still reminisce, we have now re-established our friendships in real time, not just based on the past. At least, that's the way I see it.

Lawee clearly forgave me as my husband and I went to his wedding. After 34 years with his wonderful lady, two children and two grandchildren, they got married and we were there to see it and share their very special day.

Back to School

30th March 2017. A day to remember.

One of our friends who was working at Menzies contacted us to let us know that the school was in the process of being demolished and rebuilding was ongoing. Our old school buildings were tired and falling apart. As a last farewell one of the current teachers arranged for old pupils to go and have a wander around the old school blocks before the demolition team flattened and erased it all. There were 10 of us in total from our year, and we all arrived and met in the school hall. 'A' block.

10 years after I left school, I organised a reunion. It wasn't a normal thing to do in those days and with no social media or computer technology I went to the school office and told them what I wanted to do and asked if they still had the class registers from our year. They did, and lent them to me so that I could get in touch with people. No data protection in those days either, so with names and addresses as well as phone numbers where available, I set about phoning and visiting people.

Although lots of people had moved on, most of the addresses were still home to the parents of my school friends and with very little effort I was soon able to contact lots of people.

We were allowed to use the school hall and I hired a mobile bar. We had background music on cassette of the music we had grown up with and I also invited some of our old teachers.

10 years on, we had a lovely evening and everyone who came enjoyed the evening. Unfortunately, the photo's I had have been lost in the intervening years, but I remember it well.

One girl who had been a bit intimidating for lots of us when we were at school, phoned me as she had heard I was organising a reunion. She said she wanted to come but was scared because of how she had been at school. She wanted to let me know she was reformed, married with two children and lived a very sensible life. I told her to come and enjoy the evening and not to worry.

Meantime several people had asked if she was going as even after 10 years, they had felt nervous about meeting up. I said she wasn't going and encouraged them to come. I'm really glad I did as when everyone finally met on the night it laid a few ghosts to rest for everyone.

The next time I went back was in my late 30's and bumped into the then current headmaster at church, who had been head of Geography when I was at school. He invited me to go down to school and said he would take me around. I went a week or two later, saw a few of my old teachers, who amazingly remembered me, and had another lovely nostalgic day.

This time, however, we all knew it was going to be the last time any of us could ever go back to see the school. The buildings held all the memories I could ever have wished for. Being with my group of friends was even more fun as we went from block to block and peered into the classrooms where we had spent so many hours learning together.

The Hall, 'A' block as it was known seemed very small. The organ and lectern were still there. The headmaster's carved chair was also there but looked nowhere near as imposing as it had when we were schoolchildren. Fittingly, the last headmaster's name carved on it was Mr Harrison, our headmaster. I think he was a nice man. He never seemed to be anything other than calm and measured from memory, unlike his deputy who had the very squeaky shoes and a sharp Scottish tongue.

The hall itself was looking a bit grim and tired, but as we sat waiting to be escorted around, I looked up and saw a sign about the donation of the sound equipment which had been on the wall since we were there. It was a sign that had stood the test of time and looked exactly the same as it did the day we left. It made me think of all the times we stood in the hall at assemblies and as we got older and moved up the ranks sitting at the back of the hall by the 5th year, it reminded me of the countless times I had read the sign as my mind wandered from listening to Mr Harrison and daydreamed about other things.

Leaving the hall, we went to 'B' and 'C' block. They were four stories high. Linked together on the second floor by a now disused walkway bridge each block also had a bridge from the road. These were also now disused. We would often meet our friends 'on the bridge.'

Walking in was like going back in time. Nothing much had changed, the stairs still had the same sound as we ran up and down, well, we walked more than ran nowadays, and the classrooms still looked the way they did when we had been having lessons in them. Geography, Maths, English, Art, R.E, to name a few and I felt like it was yesterday. It even smelt exactly how I remembered it.

It was the last time I was going to have the opportunity to swing from the pole on the stairs that ran from top to bottom. At school I used to love it. I would swing around the pole, land half way down the next flight of stairs and then jump to the next pole and swing around that in the same way. It meant I could get from the top floor to the bottom only stepping on 8 stairs jumping from one set of stairs to the other, bag on my shoulder for added thrust. Thankfully, I never misjudged it and never fell.

Mindful that I might not have the strength in my arms, let alone the confidence, Deana watched me from below, camera in hand as I made a very feeble attempt at swinging around the pole. I had a couple of tries and I was convinced, given enough time, I could have got better at it! Deana found it very funny as I failed! Nonetheless, it was fun and having spent many years thinking about how much fun I had doing it when I was at school, it finally laid to rest my curiosity to do it 'just one more time.'

Moving around the floors, we remembered so many things we had done. Memories abounded and as we came to the ground floor in 'C' block, I peered into my first form registration classroom. We laughed at the fact that as a Trojan, we didn't win as many prizes as some of the other houses, and I had some photos taken of me trying to look sad.

Since the building was going to be imminently demolished, I did something I never did at school and wrote a little bit of graffiti to go down with the ship. On the girls toilet wall, I wrote '79'ers Along with the date. I suspect it was the last graffiti written on 'C' block walls and I'm glad to know I left a mark of our existence.

Moving to 'D' block, which was languages, in our day the block seemed very new and modern. Now it looked faded and jaded but the sound of our footsteps on the stairs brought back more memories as being an open staircase, they had a particular 'ring' to them.

The rooms there were just as I remembered them and one in particular sparked a memory for me that has stayed with me all my life.

Another English teacher, Mr Backhouse, who was also the Trojan Housemaster, taught me for a time. I remember one lesson he was telling us about when he was in the second world war. He had a recurring dream about being attacked by a German soldier. Every time he had the dream, he was on the floor with the German soldier standing over him with his bayonet fixed ready to kill him. He would wake up in a hot sweat and feel upset for the day following. Eventually he decided he needed to change this experience and made his mind up to change it.

He said he practiced imagining a different end to the dream and changing it so he would kill the soldier instead. It took him quite a time, but eventually, he changed his subconscious to a point where one night he had the

213

dream and this time, turned the tables. As he was attacked by the soldier, he fought back and stabbed him with the bayonet instead. Having killed the soldier, he never had the dream again.

I listened in complete fascination and wondered if I could do the same with some of my dreams. After around 40 years of practice, I can say that yes, I have learned to influence several of my dreams to make them less stressful and one very happy recurring dream in particular is that I have now learned to fly properly in my dreams. When I was young, it was hard to run and take off the ground and get nowhere fast, but over the years I learned to fly, and only recently, I had a wonderful dream where I was flying so well, I could go as fast as I wanted to, fly for as long as I wanted, and it was all so very easy.

The North Revisited

As I write, we have just come out of the most remarkable time in the world. We have so far survived the Covid pandemic, the world is still in turmoil with so much going on, and for most of us, our peaceful lives have been disrupted to some degree by all the events.

Some of the positives for me are that I have rediscovered my love of embroidery, writing, (I kept a daily diary of events unfolding,) walking and also just being still.

During Covid, I saw something on TV where someone said every time they thought. saw or heard of something they wanted to do, they wrote it down on paper and put it in a bowl. I thought it was a great idea and started to do the same. One thing I wrote was to take Graham to Yorkshire in the summer, to prove the sun shone there and see it at it's beautiful best. We also wrote to go to the Kelpies and Falkirk wheel.

So, this summer, I arranged a 10 day route and off we went. We couldn't have picked a better time to go. We have had the most glorious summer. The sun didn't stop shining and everywhere looked fabulous.

I drove, as I wanted Graham to see the beauty that I remembered without being distracted. We weren't disappointed.

We arrived at Falkirk and a fabulous hotel with wonderful staff and amazing food. We went on the Falkirk wheel and also visited the Kelpies. Unbroken blue skies and sunshine accompanied us at all times. We went to Edinburgh Castle, The Royal Yacht, and visited the church where later in the year our glorious late Queen Elizabeth was taken for a service of thanksgiving.

We then drove to Northumberland. Memories of travels with Mum, Dad and Chris, flooded back. We visited Bamburgh Castle, the Grace Darling museum, Seahouses, Alnwick Castle, Dunstanburgh, Craster and lots of places en route.

Graham did say at one point he was feeling 'Castled out!' so he definitely got the proper Skidmore experience!

We then drove to Pickering, spent an afternoon with our friends who were up there too, and for the last day, I gave Graham free choice of where we went. He chose Filey. We both love it there. We walked 8 miles along Filey Brigg and the beach, before a lovely meal and returned home next day on what was one of the hottest days on record. It was one of the best holidays we have ever had, we walked over 40 miles, travelled 966 miles and filled my heart with immeasurable joy to be able to share some more of my childhood memories with my lovely Graham.

God Bless David Harris

The last word goes again to David Harris.

Sadly, during the writing of this book, David passed away. We didn't see much of each other, but he remained a constant source of happiness in my mind and heart.

He called me one afternoon and invited me to his birthday party. I said yes, I would love to go. He said,

'Well actually, it's also a goodbye party. I'm very poorly.'

Walking into the venue, we just hugged one another. We both sobbed a little, took some photos, and I will forever treasure that evening, the warmth of the hug and the memories he gave me.

At his funeral, I stood with 3 other school friends at the back of the crematorium and felt proud to be there, all grown up, but still children at heart.